LIFE WITHOUT A ZIP CODE
Travels of an American Family
in Greece and New Zealand

The University of Oklahoma

DR. ANDREW S. HORTON, DIRECTOR
THE JEANNE H. SMITH PROFESSOR
FILM AND VIDEO STUDIES PROGRAM

640 Parrington Oval, Old Science Hall 302, Norman, OK 73019
PHONE: (405) 325-0792 FAX: (405) 325-7135
E-MAIL: ahorton@ou.edu WEBSITE: www.andyhorton.org

Library of Congress Control Number 131515
ISBN: 0-918266-40-8

Printed in the United States of America

LIFE WITHOUT A ZIP CODE
Travels of an American Family in Greece and New Zealand

Andrew Horton

CONTENTS

DEDICATION

For

Penny, Costas, Kallissa and Poppy

"I've been given my incantations—
to make visible who was invisible."

Patricia Grace
A Maori New Zealand author

"The things that can be seen, heard
and learned are what I prize
the most."

Heraclitus

STARTING UP

"He who does not travel does not know the value of men."
Moorish proverb

Pick up, pack up, and GO.

But first there had been the decision to take to the open road: "Wouldn't it be crazy to take a year off and travel around the world with our children?"

"Yes," Odette, my wife replied as we sat in our 1836 Creole cottage near the French Quarter in New Orleans.

"OK, so shall we do it?"

"Why not!"

"Then let's go."

Well, it wasn't quite that easy, but what follows is an informal record of an American family taking time off from routine as we had known it and hitting the road from July 1997 to June 1998, for twelve countries, but with long stays in places: a Greek island and New Zealand. More precisely, Odette, my then twelve-year-old son Sam, seven-year-old daughter Caroline and I enjoyed five distinct odysseys. The first was a summer voyage across the United States from New Orleans to California and back. The second involved an autumn sojourn through Europe, including England, France, Italy, Slovenia, Croatia, Yugoslavia, Hungary, and the Former Yugoslav Republic of Macedonia. The third focused on Greece where we lived on the island of Kea for several months. The next was the return from Greece through Italy, Switzerland, Germany, France and England, and the final one was our six-month stay in New

Zealand from January (high summer down under!) to June, their high winter.

Family.

Friends.

Travel.

All three are celebrated and explored in these pages, which detail only the Greek and New Zealand travels.

But there is more. What follows is also about experiencing what is new and different, strange and often unexpectedly pleasing. Travel and living abroad have always been important to me. As a child in a military family, I lived in England for three years, and after college I traveled widely in Europe and South America. I had eventually lived in Greece for more than a total of eight years, and as a university professor of film studies, I have spent long stretches of time in Eastern Europe, especially the former Yugoslavia and in the former Soviet Union.

Such a scenario wouldn't work in most job situations, of course. But that is not to say that those outside the academic world cannot find a plan that can make time off possible. The hardest decision was exactly the first: *To take a full year off and travel. Period.*

Caroline was the most fearless traveler of the lot. But at one point in our family planning sessions she brushed her blond hair out of her pleasingly chubby face and began to cry, "I will miss my ROOM and toys," she said.

Sam, who became a teen during the journey, had his reservations too: "I don't want to leave my friends for so long," he said. "Can't one of them come over to Greece or New Zealand to visit?" he asked, also near tears.

"We'll be back to New Orleans in December," reasoned Odette, clearing away the Popeye's fried chicken and Cajun rice we had been eating. "And you'll make new friends along the way," she tried to say cheerfully as Sam took off to practice on his electric guitar. "That's not the same," was his reply. "But I do love Greece. Why don't we just spend the whole year there?" "Hey," I added as I looked through my shelves of video tapes, trying to decide which comedy—Keaton or Chaplin—to show in class the next day. "This is our chance to see a lot of countries you've read about. I mean, the Beatles came from ENGLAND!" But Sam was already into his version of "Norwegian Wood" and Caroline was back in her room with her American Girl doll.

Many more such high level negotiations took place over a period of months. But once we had finally decided on the "year away" plan—and it was to a large degree a family decision—the multitude of details that needed to be worked out began to make sense. Thus we faced the issue of home education for Sam and Caroline on the Greek island of Kea. And in New Zealand we placed them in a local Wellington school during those months. And we worked out how we could pay the bills with our gypsy mobile list of addresses. We also began to figure out how to make e-mail become an important partner in this nomadic existence.

Yet we had another more important "variable" to deal with. At the same time we had taken the decision to spend a year abroad, an exciting new job offer came up for me at the University of Oklahoma. The opportunity was, finally, too good to turn down and this threw us into much confusion: could we continue with our planned year? After several weeks of deliberation, all became clear: we would take the year off as planned and move to Oklahoma afterwards.

One other wish emerged as a goal for all of us: the pursuit of simplicity. A Kazakh Russian film director friend of mine, Rachid Nougmanov, had often made it clear to me over the years that Kazakhs are nomads and as such comfortable with travel and travelling light. As he has often told me, "If it doesn't fit on one camel, get rid of it." We wanted to learn more about the virtues of such simplicity.

All this said, we started packing. What follows is not a diary or a journal but rather, in the Kazakh spirit of simplicity, a sampling of our life on a Greek island and in Wellington, New Zealand for a year. LIFE WITHOUT A ZIP CODE.

Our overall spirit during our travels?

Flash forward several months into our journey to the day we

were approaching the Yugoslav border. As we drove through Slovonia, that part of Croatia under United Nations protection after the Bosnian war, Sam was first to notice the UN signs on the side of the pothole marked highway. In several languages there were warnings to BEWARE OF UNEXPLODED MINES. Having lived in New Orleans all his life, Sam was confused for just a playful instant. "What is an unexploded *mime*?" asked Sam. Odette, our seven-year-old daughter, Caroline, and I all burst into laughter. The image of "unexploded mimes" standing silently by the highway as we traveled by became a favorite memory for us as we undertook a year-long odyssey through eleven countries near the end of the 20th century.

And what would an exploded mime result in? Laughter and joy being spread everywhere? The destruction of things as they were? The interjection of a carnival spirit into routine? Certainly we all agreed that an unexploded mime represented the EAGER POTENTIAL for mischief and fun, a healthy and imaginative invitation to live fully. In fact, this image became more than a memory: it emerged as a theme for our entire adventure. Thus, Dear Reader, you are warned that you may be surprised, to say the least, by some of the "alleged" conversations recorded and characters met in these pages. All should be taken in the spirit of exploded mimes.

Norman, Oklahoma
May 2000

PART ONE
LIFE ON THE ISLAND OF KEA

"Why has the pleasure of slowness disappeared?"
Milan Kundera, *Slowness*

"Call in the inspired bard,
Demodocus. God has given the man the gift of song,
To him beyond all others, the power to please,
However the spirit stirs him on to sing."

Odysseus in Homer's *The Odyssey*

OUR ISLAND IN THE SUN

"I can see Kea!" Caroline shouted with glee.

Sam had already spotted the island we all love so well in his happy wanderings of the ferry boat from Lavrion, the mainland port some forty miles south of Athens.

It was the late Friday afternoon boat, and even though this was September 20, a full month after the tourist season, the boat was crowded with that new Greek phenomenon: the "weekenders from Athens," those professionals with enough money to build their get-away weekend houses on "our" island.

A cool breeze was blowing, and Odette was smiling with anticipation as our island home came into view. Kea was the island I have been coming to for over twenty years and which Odette and I, and now the children, have shared so many summer memories. This included part of our honeymoon, and, ten years ago, a sabbatical fall when Sam was two.

I was smiling too. But I couldn't help brushing aside a tear. Our American and European odysseys were splendid. Yet there was the immediate feeling that Kea was what we were aiming for, and here, in all its Aegean glory, before us, it called to us.

"You made it!" said Judy, our American artist friend who has been living in Greece for thirty years and whose island home we would be staying in up in the main village, Hora.

"And I feel very SPOILED this time!" I managed.

"What do you mean?" asked Tim, Judy's husband, a solidly built American who teaches physical education in the American Community School of Athens, the same school where Judy, a well respected artist in her own right, has been teaching art for years.

"Spoiled because this time we have a CAR!" I laughed.

And I had a flash of years of waiting for buses that didn't come, of trying to reach busy island taxi drivers through phone calls to their wives and even of hitchhiking with farmers in the back of Nissan or Toyota pickup trucks, sitting with sheep or tomatoes and bricks. Now that we were closer, the weekenders were buzzing happily as the new whitewashed homes built in the past few years and splashed along the rocky coast came into view.

Kea, a member of the Cycladic islands, some fifteen miles off the coast, roughly fifteen miles long and about six miles wide, with a population of under two thousand permanent residents. Farming has always been the main occupation, but in recent years the building boom for the weekenders has turned almost everyone into a real estate agent and builder as well. The isolated island I loved so much twenty years ago is still a joy, but it is now a shared joy, especially on weekends but even in summers when French, British, German and Scandinavian tourists crowd the beaches and seaside tavernas.

Many islanders we recognized waved or came over to greet us. There was no surprise on their faces. Only the gentle smile and "hello," as if we had not been "away," but simply in Athens for a spell and now returning "home" again.

And then we rounded the rocky cape that hides the port from approaching ships and Korrissia, the harbor village sprang into view.

"There's Stephanos and Katerina!" Sam shouted, waving furiously.

And so they were.

Stephanos runs a fine gift shop on the harbor, is a talented short story writer, and, as of the past year, had become the mayor of the island. Earlier in the year I had arranged his visit to New Orleans during Mardi Gras where he gave a lecture on his fiction and Greek prose today. He had returned with the spirit and memory of carnival to face the problems of governing an island facing all the excitement and confusion of great change. Katerina, his vivacious and intelligent wife, is from northern Greece and has with her good humor and great hospitality been a true friend as well.

The happy chaos of disembarking was compounded this time as I drove our trusty Peugeot we had rented in Paris and driven through Italy and the former Yugoslavia out of the hull of a ferry stuffed with huge construction trucks and a myriad of weekend small Renaults, Russian Niva jeeps, and pickup trucks stuffed with furniture and even large plants hanging over the sides.

By the time I elbowed our car out behind a killing cloud of diesel fumes, Sam, Caroline, and Odette were already climbing into Stephanos' car as embraces were given all around. Meanwhile Tim and Judy loaded their spear fishing gear into our car for the four-mile drive up the mountain to The Village.

"Welcome home!" beamed Stephanos.

And he meant it.

HOME IN HORA

That evening I drove the four miles along the winding ascending road to Hora, the main village of the island, our home for the next two months. Rounding a bend and seeing that whitewashed gathering of houses spread out across the side of a mountain worked its old magic: what a place, what a view.

Usually we would in the past take the bus and then hike the hundred plus stone steps up to Judy's home. For life in Hora is one of up and down on stone with only a few short stretches of STRAIGHT! This time, however, we really felt spoiled. I could drive the upper road above the village, park, and walk down a hundred steps, loaded like a Kea mule with our suitcases, to reach the grape vine covered balcony of Judy's place.

Sam, Caroline and Odette were already there when I arrived and a mini carnival was in progress.

"Look, Caroline, our flippers and beach towels!" Sam called out digging through one of several bags pulled from storage. "And, Sam, some of my old books, remember?" Caroline happily yelled in discovery, as Odette continued to pull several suitcases out of the closet.

That night we feasted in the main square at Yannis' taverna and celebrated with Judy and Tim our homecoming. "Now that we sold our New Orleans home," Sam said with mixed joy and nostalgia. "Kea really is my home."

And so it was.

I don't remember what time we went to bed, for there was the continued pleasure of rediscovery as we settled in to our island home, which was composed of an upstairs room with a kitchen in one corner, a fireplace in the other, a table and two stone bench ledges that were Sam's and Caroline's beds by night. Oh, and a Franklin stove which we ignored until the temperature dropped.

Down the stone steps were our bedroom and a short hallway with the bathroom branching off of it and a downstairs door to the outside as well.

In a word, small, but somehow, once we had unpacked and put away, Judy's house was a home with everything we needed.

"And my guitar is here!" Sam said.

Sam and I had brought several suitcases and the guitar in May when I had come with a comedy study group from the States, and so we were lucky we did not have to lug winter clothes and extra books and a guitar around Europe.

"Will you teach me to play too, Sam?" asked Caroline as we put out the lights. "We'll see," yawned Sam.

And then the silence of the island. Broken only by the sound of an occasional owl or donkey somewhere in the distance.

BULLETS IN THE GAS TANK

A mountain village without cars. Thus no noise and no bullets in our gas tank. It takes a place like Kea to remind us what we all learn to "put up with" in our regular daily lives. We loved our New Orleans 1836 home, a Creole cottage we had painstakingly restored. But besides three break-ins in twelve years, there was the night we heard noise outside and couldn't tell if it was gunfire or fireworks. Both were common in our mixed middle and lower class old neighborhood that was about half black and white.

The next morning when the car wouldn't start, Sam noticed gas under the car, and we called AAA to tow the car to a nearby garage. It wasn't an hour before we got a call: "Found the problem. Bullet in the gas tank. You're lucky it didn't blow up on 'ya. Guess you didn't have the engine on or it would have been one hell of an explosion. Would have killed you, of course!"

We laughed and then became frightened. Those stray neighborhood bullets could have hit Sam or Caroline, not to mention us. And even if they hadn't, a running motor would have meant a fireball ending.

The quiet nights of Kea spoke loudly about the noise of our American home.

ARGIRIS AND VASSO

"Welcome, Andreas!" called out Argiris, giving me a bear hug.

"I'll get you a coffee," beamed Vasso, as she in turn embraced me warmly.

It felt good to see the friends we had known longest on the island again.

Together they had, for more than twenty years, run the small taverna they still sit in front of every day to sip coffee, talk with friends walking by and to take a break from working in their general grocery store across the narrow street.

They were, simply put, family for us. And the memories of evenings spent in their old taverna since Sam was two and, later, with Caroline, are some of our happiest ever.

Argiris is from a simple farm down at the tip of the island where his deaf brother, Costa, still lives, with one of the best views of the Aegean but without running water or electricity, tending the sheep. In his 50s, Argiris has a strongly etched face with a warm smile and a shock of thick nearly white hair.

Vasso is a pleasantly large woman from the Peloponnese, with eyes that sparkle and a ready laugh that cuts through any problems they or friends may be facing. One glance at them both and one knows they will never run out of unexploded mimes.

And so one happy island ritual began again: sitting with a rich thick medium sweet Greek coffee, *metreo*, and catching up on the shape of the world.

"What's new?" I asked in Greek since they know no English. "We will be grandparents in a month!" beamed Vasso.

"Great! Congratulations! How is Eiriene?" I ask about their married daughter in Athens. Time thus begins to slip by pleasantly and, sometimes, painfully as the conversation flows.

"We had some big problems this summer," said Argiris coming back from serving a customer in the shop. "Twenty of Argiris' sheep were slaughtered at Petroussa (the family home)," adds Vasso suddenly shedding her smile.

"What?" I say, not believing my ears.

"Came by motor boat, goddamn them, shot and skinned them, taking only the meat and left." Argiris looks ten years older as he says this.

"On Kea? How possible?" My image of Kea as a kind of paradise outside the problems of the real world begins to shatter.

"Possible. And maybe an inside island job since they must have known that Costa is deaf," adds Vasso.

I was home with friends. And that, I realized immediately, meant sharing their grief as well as their joys.

TOILETS GREEK, TURKISH, AND AMERICAN!

Greek toilets can be a surprise to Americans who are unaware of Aegean plumbing. Of course Turkish johns are even more surprising. I mean, of course, those WC's with a hole in the floor and porcelain footprints to stand on and, well, aim and fire away.

Fortunately we had a sit down toilet at Judy's, but it was "Greek" in the sense that a small covered waste bin was next to the toilet for the depositing of all used papers.

Odette read to us frequently from that delightful ageless "comic non fiction" book, Gerald Durrell's *My Family and Other Animals*. Of course Durrell kept us all roaring with laughter in his description of growing up on Corfu with his fatherless British family in the 1930s. But I had forgotten that he kicks it all off with the British horror of Greek toilets. Here is brother Lawrence (Larry) Durrell explaining all to his sister once they arrive in Greece:

> "Owing to the somewhat eccentric plumbing system of the town," he explained to Margo kindly, "that little box is provided for the . . . er . . . debris, as it were, when you have finished communing with nature." (24)

Oh, yes, and nothing has changed since then! But one Greek friend did give us a different perspective on "the little covered waste basket." Her claim was that this whole tradition got started because Greeks used to use old newspapers for toilet paper and, "Of course, THAT wouldn't flush!" Now, however, with super soft paper everywhere, it's not really a problem, "But like adding retsin to wine to make retsina still, it's just a habit to keep on using that little covered waste basket long after its need has vanished!"

Our days on Kea flowed by pleasantly, and, despite such glowing reports about improved plumbing and paper, we kept our little covered basket, feeling we were part of a great tradition of paper savers!

MY FIRST CONVERSATION WITH HOMER

I was on my favorite jogging route on Kea from Hora to the Port via the old stone path that used to be the main road before cars came into the picture. One of the pleasures of this little used trail is that you do have it all to yourself. So imagine my surprise to see an old fellow in a toga sitting under an olive tree plucking a lyre and humming to himself.

"Hello," he called out in Greek as I jogged by. This brought me to a sweaty halt as I stopped to reply.

"Are you headed to a costume party or is Greek television shooting a special?" I asked in the best Greek I could.

He chuckled and his eyes were unblinking and did certainly

did not focus on me. "No, I'm just doing what I always do," he replied, beginning to strum again.

"And who exactly are you?"

"Oh, I go by various names. Some simply call me the Bard, others say Demodocus, but I prefer Homer."

I almost fell. "*Homer?* You? But that's not possible. Homer died over two thousand years ago. I'm afraid you've been in the sun too long and…"

The old man put down his lyre and offered me an olive from a bowl beside him. "It's convenient for folk to believe I'm dead," he said quietly. "But I'm still singing my songs and strumming my lyre for those who wish to hear," he added while petting a sheep which hand wandered in front of him.

"Well, it's just not possible. Period. That's all."

I took an olive and waved a hand in front of his eyes. He did not blink.

"I'm not trying to convince anyone, young man. By the way, you have an accent. Where are you from?"

"New Orleans for the past twenty years," I said, wondering where this was all going.

"Ah! New Orleans! Far from windy Troy's high walled citadels," he quipped as he held out his hand as if he wanted me to help pull him up.

Which I did.

"You know New Orleans?"

"Louis' city! An epic place." he said, slinging his lyre over his shoulder and picking up a walking staff.

" 'Louis' as in Louis Armstrong?"

"Exactly. When we were singing together one night about good times and bad times, about wars won and lost, love found and destroyed, we realized what kindred souls we are. After all, we both sing stories that people everywhere want to hear apparently." He began down the path and I walked beside him.

"Wait. Let's back up. You are Homer and you are a friend of

Louis Armstrong and…" The old man was humming to himself again, but this time I realized it was Armstrong's great song, "It's a Wonderful World."

I felt I was losing my grip, so I broke out into the first line of *The Odyssey*, "Sing, Goddess, of the Man of Many Ways," and the old man immediately took it from there, singing his lines softly in a hypnotic chant.

I bent to tie an unruly lace and when I stood, the old man was gone.

But faintly in the distance I heard that humming and I began to smile too.

When I got back to the house, I was humming too.

"What's that song?" Odette asked.

"Oh, a little thing I picked up from an old man on the path." I paused and smiled. "It's called Lyre Lyre."

And we sat down to a feta cheese omelet.

LAUGHING THROUGH THE ISLANDS

Back in late May, bagpipe music rang out of the Monastery of Kastriani's old dinning room. Leftheris, one of the three priests on the island, played his homemade bagpipe and one of his lovely teenage daughters kept beat on a drum. Irene, his other daughter, led Nick in an island dance as other members of my seminar on Comedy entitled, "Laughing Out Loud," joined in too. Nick is our British writer friend who is working in Hollywood.

We were spending the night in the monastery at the beautiful but isolated north end of the island, high on a cliff overlooking the sea and the island of Andros in the distance.

But this academic study group—the eighth I had led to Greece as part of offerings of The Aegean Institute, a study and travel program I had developed—was different. This dance evening was actually part of an ongoing wedding feast. Two members of my group, Ken and Polly, had chosen to be married on Kea during the trip. And a wonderful wedding it had been. After months of faxes and paperwork to complete all the Greek requirements for a civil marriage, they lived out their dream and a civil marriage was held in the beautiful neo classical town hall in the center of Hora. (A church wedding was not possible because they were not Orthodox.)

The wedding was attended by all in the group, who, given that our focus was on comedy, were in the right mood. Adella Adella, a professional New Orleans story telling friend, helped lead us in a jazzy set of tunes from "Going to the Chapel" to "Stop in the Name of Love" as the vice mayor of the island led the Greeks in some rousing versions of old Greek songs. Wine and food filled the main conference room of the town hall as Stephanos in his role as mayor pronounced them man and wife in Greek and English.

The dancing to bagpipe and drums in the monastery was almost literally the icing on the cake.

Of course as the days went by for us in the fall, I had many such pleasant memories of groups I had brought to Kea in the past and the strongly pleasing effect it had had for many. This included Melanie, who had enjoyed Greece and Kea so much on one trip that she wound up coming on three of my journeys and even naming her daughter Kea.

LAST ONE INTO THE SEA IS A ROTTEN...

I was catching my breath on the almost empty beach at Yaliskari. Then Odette came into view driving, and I had fun rubbing it in that I had beat them down, jogging the five miles from Hora on the mountain all the way to our favorite beach.

"Last one into the sea is a rotten *souvlaki*," I said, and the rush for the water began. We had a good solid month of swimming on Kea, long past the tourist season, much to our delight. That balmy September weekday afternoon there were a couple of Scandinavians and one or two Greeks on late holiday. And that was it. By October we had the beaches to ourselves every day. On weekends Judy and Tim often joined us until the weather really turned. They would get out all their underwater wet suit fishing gear and disappear for several hours at a time at the various beaches we drove to, including Spathi on the back side of the island and a most isolated one behind the harbor at Aghia Irini that we hiked to.

One time they came back with an octopus that became my first and only octopus feta omelet, and another day Judy showed up with one hell of a large eel that she had already beheaded.

Odette and I never tired of watching Sam and Caroline, sharing a mask but each with fins, conducting their own underwater searches and endless games that the still warm Aegean invited them to play.

It was a sad day in October when it began to pour—the first rain of winter—and we made a mad dash away from the beach, realizing our swimming days were numbered.

THE LITTLE WHITE KEA SCHOOL HOUSE

"Everybody out of bed," I called out. "You have to go to SCHOOL today." Sam and Caroline both groaned, turned over and muttered something about it was "too early yet." I had a quick reply: "Early? No! You actually have been able to sleep an hour later than when you are in the States because you don't have to leave home, so let's get movin'!"

And so school began on our third day on Kea, a bright but chilly September Monday. But instead of a little red schoolhouse on a hilltop as in children's books, we were the tiny white schoolhouse in a Greek island village.

Of all the difficulties we had considered before beginning our voyage, I think "home schooling" was the most daunting. For all of our initial enthusiasm for the idea, would we really be able to carry it out in practice? After all, it's hard enough to be a parent, but add to this the task of being their TEACHER, and we would double the possibilities Sam and Caroline would flee off into the mountains never to return!

Yet that sunny Monday morning and afternoon relieved our fears swiftly. Our months of travels including the museums and historical locations, the discussions, the talks with friends and car readings of books had all had their positive effect. So by 8:30 Sam and Caroline, with a good deal of joking about the "first day of school," showed up "in class" by clearing their cereal bowls, gathering their notebooks, and having a seat on cushions on the floor facing Odette. She sat on Sam's couch and began a math and logic lesson with plastic colored blocks of various shapes and sizes.

School had begun!

While down below in our bedroom, I worked away on my own project for the year—a book contracted by the University of California Press on comic screenplay writing for film and television—I was impressed by the frequent outbursts of laughter as Caroline and Sam attacked their assignments with good humor and shared enthusiasm.

As the weeks wore on we worked out a variety of approaches to home education. Sometimes Odette and me took one or the other of the children off separately for a specific "lesson," turned visitors into guest lecturers, or had them write up special "investigations" we gave them to do in the village. This included finding out how a bakery works, spending time with Stephanos the mayor in his office, and, of course, taking Greek lessons with Katerina.

But our method for the home schooling term was simple and one well established by others who have promoted the concept: three hours of close supervised home schooling easily covers the seven hours students spend in school. For within those seven hours one must immediately subtract lunch time, physical education, study hall and other activities that are not academic per se. Our three hours of "class," of course, represented only the base. To that we would have to count a lot more of the day, perhaps giving "school" work some ten hours a day, if we factored in two or three hours a day for swimming or hiking, the evening reading of Homer, the time to write in their journals and the half hour or so they devoted to their own reading.

In the days that followed there were lows as well as highs. Sam often felt frustrated and threatened to board a plane for New Orleans to join his friends at his old school.

"I'd give ANYTHING to be back in my old school," he said one day in tears, realizing that in New Orleans he had often said he would give anything not to go to school. But perhaps what impressed me most about the flow of the school days on Kea was the GOOD HUMOR.

Nothing ever sounded better to my ears than Sam and Caroline laughing together as they worked jointly on a project. And more often than not, it was laughter that carried over into our activities throughout the day and into the evening. The Navaho Indians speak of "holy laughter" in their religious ceremonies. And on Kea, I found my children's laughter to be, if not holy, truly the laughter of shared discovery and joy.

THE TERRACED LANDSCAPE

Nothing speaks more eloquently on Kea of the human touch through the years than the terraced landscape.

Literally everywhere you look there are mountains, and all are terraced.

Because of the rocky uneven land, such a technique has always been the only way to maximize the farming and grazing potential of the island. Often for the fun of it on Kea, I would gaze off at a mountain and start to count how many narrow—usually no more than say 12-20 feet wide—terraces sliced through the landscape. And seldom would I count fewer than twenty while other mountains have over thirty.

Think what that means. Each terrace painstakingly constructed by piling countless stones, leveling off soil, planting or not planting for some was clearly meant merely to hold sheep or goats or cows, and creating small stone steps up to the next terrace. Of course most are in disuse now, mere ghostly reminders of a time when the island had thousands more in population and when the whole island was alive with micro-farming. What I wouldn't give to have a brief flashback to what it was like then, and to date I've found no photos of those more fertile periods.

"I've been to China and just about everywhere else," said our friend John Tirrell, a globetrotter from an early age and an American working in the cruise and travel business in Athens for over thirty years. "But I've never seen terracing like this anywhere!"

It was his first visit to Kea, and we had taken him clear around the island. That October night we toasted John's visit and the terraces of Kea!

MORNING COFFEE WITH THE BOYS

It didn't take long for me to set into a morning rhythm.

An early riser, I enjoyed my first cup of coffee reading in bed, everything from Milan Kundera to Moliere, Shakespeare, modern Greek writers, to background work for the book I began writing on Kea about screenwriting and comedy. And the very early morning was also the best time for writing postcards, letters and e-mail messages.

Then after giving Sam and Caroline their 7:30 wake up song and dance, I was out of the house and down the hundred and eight steps to check my mail at the one room post office and to download and send e-mail at the phone office. This meant that by 8 a.m., I was ready to join the "boys" for a good thick medium sweet Greek coffee, called a *metreo*.

The "boys"? Well, gathered each morning either at the *kafeneon* (coffee shop) at the bus square or just inside the arch that leads into the village at another kafeneon, were a gang of four to, at one time, twenty eight fellows of all ages and walks of life. We spent half an hour to an hour catching up on the shape of the universe, not to mention the island.

There was Nikos, the bus driver who I've known for years and used for my study groups that come to Kea. And there was always at least one of the taxi drivers, including Angelos, Dimitri, and Gregorios, who had been the mayor for a number of years and who looks strikingly like Gabriel Garcia Marquez. Then some farmers, and some non-island phone company young men working on Kea temporarily. Finally, there were a few old island men with great moustaches, piercing bright eyes, and hand carved wood canes.

Almost never could I pay the 300 drachmas ($1.25) for my own coffee, for they were always treating "the professor" as most of them called me.

It's hard to think of many activities that have given me as much pleasure as just listening to these fellows chat away each day on whatever topic popped up at the moment. And they covered everything from rising real estate prices on the island, to the Greek treatment of Turkish threats, to the latest hot gossip on the island, to the latest jokes they had heard. Sometimes I was brave enough to jump in too.

"How many churches are there really on Kea?" I asked (in Greek, of course), one morning. This set them off for forty minutes!

"Four hundred," said Nikos.

"No way, Niko," said one Dimitri. "Two hundred fifty."

"Nobody knows, you fools," offered yet another. "It's more like 325 though, I'm sure."

And the minutes flew by as the question was debated, deconstructed, re-assembled, and finally, dropped with no conclusion.

"Nobody knows," shrugged Nikos with a smile.

ODYSSEUS ON KEA

"Bedtime, gang," either I or Odette would call out when 8:30 rolled around each evening. "Time for Homer-work!"

During our island stay, this was a familiar call, especially after my encounter with the old Bard that day on the way to the port.

After a full day of school and hiking or swimming or visiting with friends, we would wrap each evening with my reading from Homer's *The Odyssey* in the new Robert Fagle's translation. When Odette and I thought of lugging the large hardcover Homer over back in the States, we had no idea how well such readings might go.

But Homer turned out to be more popular than television, videos of The Simpsons, or simply playing around before turning out lights.

"Can we have a double dose of Homer if we get ready FAST?" Caroline would gleefully ask. "OK, if you pick up your mess around your bed too, Sam." And a scurry would take place.

Then snug in Odette's and my downstairs bed, the words of the bard would ring out for the next forty-five minutes:

"Alcinous!" wary Odysseus continued, "cross that thought from your mind, I'm nothing like the immortal gods who rule the skies, Either in build or breeding. I'm just a mortal man. Whom do you know most saddled down with sorrow? They are the ones I'd equal, grief for grief."

They listened with rapt attention. And often with questions along the way—"Who did you say the Cyclops' father was? Who was his mother?"—and Sam and Caroline's happy choral response every time I signaled them for the appropriate choral response.

"And when Odysseus and his crew had set aside their need…"

My cueing finger to Sam and Caroline and a football fan shout response of: "FOOD AND DRINK!" rang out.

Or, "When Dawn with her…."

Cue, and response, "ROSEY-RED FINGERS."

Sleep came easy for them after the voyages we took each night to Circe's island or to Nestor's palace with Telemachus or all the way to Ithaca as father and son at last join up for the violent finish.

MY ISLAND OFFICE

The little white schoolhouse had been rolling along every morning for a week, and I had begun to dig into my own writing. But if the truth were told, it was hard for me to concentrate on my own work while enjoying sounds of Sam and Caroline and hearing Odette conduct classes.

How to get my work done peacefully in our limited space on Kea?

Judy and Tim showed up the weekend after our first week and had the perfect solution.

"Use the other room we stay in!" Judy said, referring to a one room "apartment" below her ex-husband, Lou's, home next door.

Some fifteen steps downhill, this room had an old split door entrance, meaning you could open just the bottom half or just the top or both, a feature that tells you clearly how island homes were designed. The ground floor was reserved for animals (thus with a half door, you could lean in and throw in some hay!), while the family lived upstairs!

Judy and Tim stayed in the room when they came since we had taken over their home. But every other day, the place was my office!

A simple room with a view of the whole Aegean through its two windows facing the sea. I had my desk, a bed to spread out my "comic" papers, electricity to plug in the computer, and an electric radiator when the weather turned cool to keep me warm.

Thus with a smile and a cup of coffee, I would leave "home" each morning headed for "the office." Does work get any better? I think not!

KATERINA TEACHES GREEK

Sam poured over his notebook and began reading slowly but clearly, "*Kathi Proi troho to fagito mou kai pino to gala mou.*"

"Bravo," replied Katerina Stephanos, the mayor's wife, who had agreed to be Sam's and Caroline's Greek teacher twice a week while we were on Kea. ("And what does it mean in English?")

Caroline answered, "Every morning I eat my food and drink my milk."

"Yes," Katerina cheerfully said, reaching for slices of apple pie for each.

Seated in her lovely living room above their shop in the harbor, Sam and Caroline began to sponge up a lot more Greek than we ever expected, thanks to the generosity and energy and concern Katerina devoted to them.

"We could meet every day," Katerina had said when we began, "Because now that Stephanos is mayor, I never see him, and the shop is closed now that the season is over. So I have all the time in the world."

Odette and I counted ourselves lucky to have such a good and talented friend. And the payoff was clear every day as Sam and Caroline became more and more adventuresome in speaking Greek in shops and with Greek friends wherever we traveled.

Will Katerina ever know how great an impression she made on these two children who voluntarily poured over vocabulary and language notes in Greek!

ALBANIANS ON KEA: THE "INVISIBLE" ILLEGAL WORKERS

Razor thin, with spry step and the skin drawn tight but not unpleasantly around his face, the young man in vaguely outdated clothing, walked by me up the stone steps of a Hora lane as I was coming down with a brisk, "*Ya sou*" (Hello).

There was a slight accent and he carried a loaf of bread and a plastic sack of food purchases, most likely from Arigiris'. He was one of the estimated three hundred Albanian workers on the island.

During our Kea stay, the "Albanian issue" became one of the most fascinating topics for us in terms of changes on the island and, indeed, in Greek culture.

Think about how we Americans deal or don't deal with the whole theme of illegal Mexican residents in the United States, and you already understand what I'm about to say. Quite simply, since the fall of communism in the Balkans, 750,000 (again, an estimate since there are no records) illegal Albanians are living and working in Greece. The official government line is that they should not be in Greece and police should be rounding them up and sending them home by the busload. And, for a while, this approach was taken.

But of course it didn't work. On the one hand, the Albanians simply turned around and came back over the boarder on foot illegally at night. And on the other hand, as in the States, thousands of Greeks have taken advantage of coolie labor for which they do not have to pay social security or health insurance.

It's a fascinating set up. And to the credit of all, it appears to be something of a win-win situation at the moment. The Albanians are very good workers, they make money, they send it home, and Kea is going through a building boom as rich Athenians need their villas built and islanders want to build or remodel homes and thus a need for hands which the Greeks cannot provide.

Add to this that there is, on Kea, no crime. In Athens one hears stories of Albanians and Ukrainians and Turks and Kurds stealing this and killing here and there. But not on Kea. It is, after all, an island, and because one is confined, one behaves.

In fact, to the average tourist, the Albanians are invisible. They are quiet, they blend in, they work hard, and keep to their own after hours.

The future?

That's the rub. For sure, as in the States, the socio-economic and political implications in the future are enormous. But for the moment, all is peaceful.

"Ya sou," I said back to the young fellow as he walked past me.

CYCLADIC E-MAIL

OTE is the name for the Greek phone company meaning, in transliteration, Organization of Telephones of Ellas (Greece). And each morning, Monday through Friday, I'd leave the house before eight headed down a hundred and eight steps for the island's OTE office, just below the bakery and the new kafeneon.

There, carrying my computer, I would greet Tassos, the always smiling fellow who ran the office, climb a chair and reach up for a special extension socket and plug in for my e-mail.

Before we left New Orleans we did as much homework on international e-mail as possible, but we had no real idea if we could make it work on Kea.

We had, of course, no phone in our home. And most Greek phones still are of an old sort that have no separate plug-in attachment like those needed for computers.

But the OTE connection was perfect, and for the price of a call to our server in Athens, we were in touch with the world. And those mornings I didn't have my *"metreo"* with the guys, I'd go to the new kafeneon and plug in, sip coffee and read the ten to twenty messages a day from New Zealand, Yugoslavia, Italy, the States, including Mom and my twenty-three-year-old son, Phil, who was happily following an MA in drama at Carnigie Mellon University in Pittsburgh.

Thus I enjoyed the sound of old Greek men arguing about the price of milk and sheep while smelling thick coffee, and looking out the window at an incomparable view of the mountains and the sea beyond while reading, "Dad, I just got the part of Lysander in A Midsummer Night's Dream," or "What do Sam and Caroline want for Christmas?" or "What films do you wish to use when you are with us in Wellington?"

Thus by 8:30 I would have caught up with the world beyond Kea and on the island too before settling down for a long morning of writing in "the office."

TAVERNA HORTON

"We're almost ready!" Sam called out from the kitchen.

The house was filled with a full spicy aroma of a great penne in progress.

"Dad, can you set the table?" Chef Sam asked.

"I'll do it!" added in Caroline, intent on being Sam's assistant.

"Then I'll get the drinks," I said.

And Odette was already helping with a Greek salad. Presto! A gourmet meal prepared by Sam was ready. This was a new turn for him.

"I love cooking," he beamed, since the whole idea had been his, influenced in part by the fact we have always enjoyed cooking up mini and maxi feasts for family and friends. But also Sam had enjoyed one of the best American films in years, "Big Night," a movie about two gourmet Italian American chefs named Primo and Secundo, who run a small restaurant in New Jersey in the 1950s.

"I'm Primo," added Sam, "And Caroline is Secundo!"

What a happy feast it was too. Little did we realize that Sam had set a high standard for a lot of culinary pleasure to follow.

There was the cold October evening that Caroline reversed her role by becoming Primo and cooking a killer lentil soup that she was justly proud of.

And then there was that joyful night when Odette was brave enough to try goat stew, which she was afraid would wind up in the trash, but turned out to be one of the gastronomic highlights of the Kea stay.

BONFIRES FOR ST. PHILIPOS

A full moon was rising over the chilly Aegean, right behind the island of Tinos in the far distance. Sam threw more logs on the beach fire we had built, and Tracy, a teaching friend from New Orleans days, sat on one of the three stone seats I had proudly constructed "in the Kean style" for our evening beach party. Then Tracy pulled out his "mini-dulcimer"—a three stringed very small instrument that looks a whole lot more like a modified mandolin to me than a dulcimer—and launched into a rip roaring, country rock song, "Grandma Slept With Chuck Berry," a song he had composed based on a "true story" a musician friend had once told him.

It was a glorious night. And smack dab in the middle of October Sam and I were camping with an old teaching friend from New Orleans, Tracy, at the isolated beach of Aghios Phillipos (St. Philip).

The waves beat against the shore, the fire crackled, Tracy's music rang out playfully, and the moon illuminated all including the small chapel of St. Philip set on a cliff over the beach, complete with its stone yard and adjoining guest house.

Sam was smiling, and as I refilled my glass and Tracy's with island retsina wine, I gave Sam a hug. We were camping on Kea.

Tracy had arrived a few days earlier for a week with his wife Dina and their two daughters, Bebe, an eight-year-old friend of Caroline's, and Maggie, age three. Tracy had been at Loyola University in New Orleans when I joined the faculty, but after rather shoddy treatment by the powers-that-be, he had in recent years been teaching English at the Air Force Academy. At present, he had just begun a two-year teaching contract at the new American University of Bulgaria, some 100 kilometers south of Sofia.

It was very good to see them again. And of course Caroline was beside herself with joy to have a good friend to play with for a whole week (yes, a few days of depression set in once Bebe left).

We wandered the island together, swimming, hiking, and managing to get all eight of us into our trusty Peugeot for drives here and there. We enjoyed hearing their tales of what it is like for an American family to settle into basically small town Bulgaria today in post-communist but still pretty much a "pre-capitalistic" Balkan state. "Let's put it this way," Dina had said after visiting Argiris' general store, "Argiris' shop looks like paradise to me since the typical Bulgarian shop has almost nothing on its shelves!"

Yes, we felt all the more comfortable in our Kea environment after the tales Dina and Tracy told, but also full of admiration for what they are experiencing. "There are pluses too," Dina added. "The kids are learning Bulgarian very quickly, we do have family time and we will get to travel to a lot of places. Hey, we are in Greece!"

And we toasted them once more.

But that night on the beach Sam and I vowed to do more camping.

"I love this, Dad," Sam said, and he meant it.

That night Sam, Tracy, and I fell happily asleep in our sleeping bags under an almond tree on stone benches in the church's courtyard. We had feasted inside the guest house on simple fare: bread, cheese, sardines, fruit and cookies.

Guest house, you say? Yes, on Kea there is a tradition that these isolated family churches have adjoining guest structures, complete with, as a minimum, tables, chairs or benches, and a gas lantern or two, dishes and silverware. Just before we hiked the four miles down mountain path to the beach, we had stopped by a mountain top church, St. Simeon, I had not visited in over six years. Besides the fine view and lovely church, the "guest house" for the church had tables and seats for about fifty people—easy, and not only all the items listed above, but gas stove, electricity, coffee, sugar and a fridge ready to be plugged in. And unlocked. Ready for any stranger to stop and rest and have a meal and then travel on.

"Imagine such a concept in America," I suggested to Tracy as we finished our meal at St. Phillipos.

"Right!" laughed Tracy. "You would be stolen blind in a New York or New Orleans minute."

Behind the laughter was our sad realization of how rare this Kea hospitality really is in the world beyond Kea's shores.

KEYS IN THE DOOR

Security on Kea?

Very often people leave their keys in the door. That is, if they have locks on the doors. Most of the churches on the island still have no locks. You can simply drop in any time and light a candle and say a prayer or, for that matter, spend the night if it is one of the mountaintop or country chapels.

But even in Hora or the port, it is a common sight to see keys in the door.

Every day I would walk past Argiris' shop, and his keys were hanging. Why? Well, it's easy. You unlock the door and then why bother to take the keys out until it's time to leave?

The same was true for taking Sam and Caroline for their Greek lessons with Katerina. We would know she was home and ready for us because the keys were in the door.

"Let yourself in," was the call from within.

And, on Kea, we did.

"I'M A GRANDFATHER!"

I was coming out of the town hall one day when I saw Argiris, his hair completely disheveled, coming across the Square shouting, "I'm a grandfather! I'm a grandfather!"

His eyes beamed and he gave me a hug.

"Congratulations! When?" I said.

"Two hours ago!" And he was gone.

Odette was thrilled to hear the news too, and we realized that their daughter, Irene, must have had a Caesarian for Vasso had left the island two days earlier telling us the child would be born on the very day in October that it was born on. And, yes, it was an "operation," Argiris later confirmed. I then explained to Odette that for many women in Greece this is still the way children are born: you make a date with the doctor and the child WILL be born on that day!

We immediately thought how different a world a new friend we met on the island, Effy, had dedicated her life to. Now retired, she is a Greek who had been a midwife for years in England and had helped hundreds of women give birth naturally at home. Effy has built a lovely home just above Hora with one of the best views anywhere on the island. One night over wine and delicious hors' d 'oeuvres she told us of a New Zealand couple back in the 1960s who were staying down near the sea in the village of Pisses and wanted a home birth. Everyone, however, told them to go to a hospital in Athens, as had Vasso and Argiris' daughter. Because of legal complications, Effy could not officially assist, but she gave them what they needed for tying the cord and other helpful things. And low and behold, a beautiful daughter was born and laid in its "crib," a guitar case, that day. This was the first child born in the village in over twenty years.

The day after Argiris' granddaughter was born, I was shopping in his store and asked how mother and child were doing.

With his ever-present twinkle and chuckle he said, "Irene is in pain because of the operation, but otherwise fine. However," he laughed, "My granddaughter can't speak yet and doesn't seem to recognize me on the phone!"

I laughed and foolishly asked what they had named her, not remembering the Greek custom that Argiris answered with.

"We won't know until the baptism," he said.

For in Greece it is the custom to speak of the child as "child" or "it" until baptized, a ceremony that may not take place until the child is at least a year old.

A WELL BAKED WRITING ASSIGNMENT

It was my job to give Sam and Caroline writing instruction and assignments. This I did by making the whole village our classroom. Our usual meetings were held in the main *kafeneon* near the square in the back room where, in winter there was a heater, but in all seasons there is a striking view of the mountains. Dimitri, the young proprietor, became used to us conducting school in his coffee shop as village men argued about goats and the price for stones in the front room.

But one day we went to the two bakeries to do our work.

The assignment was to write a comparison and contrast essay. So what better way to do so than to interview the bakers at the two shops in the village.

Yannis runs the old wood burning traditional bakery near our home, and Eirene is the daughter of another old baker who basically handles her father's new bakery, which is super modern with electric ovens and lots of fancy sweets from Athens, not far from the square.

Sam and Caroline, notebooks in hand, interviewed each to the amusement of all involved. And when their essays were completed they were, I must say, well baked!

HELP US, DEAR ZEUS!

Zeus does exist!

How do I know?

Because late in October when life seemed so perfect on our adopted island, the computer crashed.

Panic.

Depression.

Followed by despair and suicidal leanings, just briefly, mind you!

Yes, somehow while working away in my Cycladic office, drops of water suddenly appeared on the keyboard. To this day I have no idea where they came from, for I did not spill anything, even though a can of club soda was on the same table. Whatever the cause, signs flashed on the computer, and then it ... crashed.

Odette and I tried everything, but to no avail. Obviously the water had gotten inside, but had it destroyed all? We didn't know. What we did understand was that we could turn it on and get the "Password" cue, but any effort to type the password ended in a shutdown.

This was lunchtime, and it was my afternoon to take Sam and Caroline out for a few hours to give Odette some needed time at home alone. You can't imagine—or maybe you can!—all the dark thoughts that stampeded through, as Homer would say, my " 'mind and heart within me.' " Yes, lots was "backed up," but a lot more was not: parts of my book, files, files and more files, not to mention e-mail info and more.

But we drove to the beautiful Hellenistic tower, one of the best preserved in Greece, at Aghia Marina, and in the lovely chapel, all three of us lit candles to that Power be he Zeus or someone else, who can hear desperate calls for help.

Then we took advantage of a partly sunny, partly warm afternoon, and the three of us plunged into the sea at the village of Pisses where we had not yet swum on this stay on the island.

Repeated tries that evening were futile. And after a filling cabbage-pasta meal, which Odette prepared, I turned in early after our Homeric reading, praying once more.

I awoke at 5:30 as usual. Put water on for coffee. And approached the computer. Pressed it on. Typed in the password. Then, surprise, it worked.

Tears of joy and a near spiritual resolution to lead a vigilant life guarding the trusty Toshiba henceforth! But, I must admit, I did have thoughts from time to time about more simple days when I would travel with my battered Hermes portable typewriter, which would never have caused me the mental and spiritual anguish this present event evoked had it fallen off a cliff or been run over by a local Toyota pickup truck! Thus the somewhat frightening realization of the dangers of living in the computer age.

SUPPER WITH SAMARAKIS

Late in October we were headed back to Kea from Athens, but I wanted desperately to see an old friend who happened to be one of the most celebrated of modern Greek writers.

Half way up Lykavitos, the mountain in the center of Athens that is higher than the Acropolis, we found his apartment building on a fashionable street. He buzzed us up when we announced ourselves at the door, and the elevator took us to the only spot on the third floor, his spacious apartment. His charming wife Eleni was first out hugging the children, and then there was Antonis, very frail now and considerably aged since I had last seen him more than a year ago. But he had his trademark pipe in hand, his playfully wise smile, and he too went for Sam and Caroline first and then Odette. Finally he grabbed my arm and with a soft, "This is the last time you will see me alive, my friend," ushered us into his life-affirming apartment with a breathtaking view of the Acropolis.

Antonis Samarakis immediately set about doing what he has always done, listening carefully to everyone, establishing a playful and lively spirit in the room, laughing loudly and pointing with deep concern to the future given the "stupidities" of governments and power structures. The room filled with others too as another noted author, Yannis Xanthoulis and his wife appeared together with Eleni's brother, Nikos and his wife Sophi, whom we have enjoyed for years and who have a lovely home in Hora.

The feast began. Antonis and Eleni's Russian maid set out dish after dish and we helped ourselves, gathering around the splendid table large enough to seat all ten of us comfortably. Laughter punctuated the devouring of the food and the pouring of the wine.

I have translated many of Antonis' ironic stories that have earned him the label as "the Greek Kafka." And as the evening flew by in laughter, bright conversation, and, as always, Antonis' focused attention on Sam and Caroline, I saluted in my mind this man who has lived a full and vibrant life, touching the lives of millions around the world.

There on one table were over a dozen different language translations of his best known work, *The Flaw*, a cautionary tale of a simple man caught in the grinding and impersonal mechanisms of a faceless totalitarian state.

"Tomorrow night at midnight turn on your TV, Andy," he said refilling my glass. "I am being interviewed and I have a few things to say about our present crazy situation in Greece."

And he went on to mention some of the many cities around Greece that had been awarding him Life Time Achievement Awards and Special Salutes for one thing or another. But really more than his writings, the awards are for him simply being himself: a concerned citizen who speaks out often and clearly and with humor, even if, given the times, it is often bitter humor.

Before we left, I was happy that I made him laugh out loud when I told him he reminded me of my favorite film director, Luis Bunuel, the Spanish surrealist.

"Bunuel once said that I want to make the most comfortable

member of the audience feel he or she is not living in the best of all possible worlds."

Antonis laughed, "Yes, my Andy, that is it! That is exactly how I feel. But do not worry yourself on Kea. You have Odette and Sam and Caroline."

WHEN WINTER BLOWS IN

The tourists always see posters of sunny Greece and lovely blue seas. But when winter blows in on Kea, another reality suddenly appears. It was late October, and the winds were so strong that the ferry boat could not run for three days. Rain mixed with clouds thus making a bone chilling damp cold. We huddled around our Franklin stove, stocking it with bought logs Judy and Tim had brought, and pick-up twigs, sticks, boards, logs Sam and I collected.

And we found ourselves automatically switching gears in a most pleasant way. Instead of protests that we weren't swimming any more, there was time to be cozy with a book or an art project or a movie Sam and Caroline hadn't seen before or one they had and loved shown on our small video playback machine I had donated several years before to the island. Thus *Clueless* was run dozens of times for Caroline and Sam got a kick out of *Witness*, old *Northern Exposure* episodes, not to mention *The Simpsons*. Yet cold weather meant more fun taking turns cooking, more time spent reading Homer, and also the beginning of long walks.

One night the rain pounded against the window, driven by a hard wind.

One last glass of local white wine and we were snuggly dug into bed for the evening.

The next morning I looked out across the terraced mountains of Kea and saw that the Greek winter miracle had happened over night. The rains and wind had stopped, and as the sun rose, the barren brown hills of the day before had suddenly become green. Winter grass had sprouted, and trees that bloom in winter such as the almond, were beginning to put forth leaves as the olives began to cry out to be harvested. New energies began to bubble for us all.

VASSO'S SEVEN COURSE FEAST

"Eat, Sam. More salad, Caroline!"

Vasso was speaking, in Greek, with a large loving smile, while pointing to her dining room table, which was groaning with food.

Odette and I gave each other knowing looks and began to dig into the feast of our lives. Argiris kept pouring the retsina while his deaf-mute brother, Costa, beamed beside him, his eyes full of years of memories of seeing Sam and Caroline grow and enjoy their family home at the far end of the island.

We knew this evening would be a real highlight in many ways.

My memories of Vasso's cooking go back over twenty years to their simple taverna in Hora, which they have now shut down. But on her "home ground," she was even more formidable. There were literally seven courses spread before us, ranging from the freshest mousaka we had ever had, pork steaks, beef in an onion and tomato stew sauce, rich spicy meatballs, a pasta and lamb dish, Greek salad, a rice salad dish that Vasso had learned from Odette several years before, and the list went on and on.

And with the food, there was the laughter.

Not to mention that Odette, Sam, and Caroline managed enough Greek that the conversation flowed along with the food and the drink and the fruits and sweets that were served as midnight fast approached.

How long to prepare all of this?

Vasso had seen me the day before and said, "Why don't you all come up tomorrow night for a little bite to eat?" And so we did!

THE LONG WINTER HIKE

"What are those bright red signs with the number one on them?" Sam asked, pointing to another small enamel painted metal sign attached to a stone wall.

Effy laughed and said, "They were put up this summer by those bright young students from around Europe who were working on Kea." Effy, in her sixties had more energy and stamina than anyone in their twenties, had hiked Mt. Olympus, the legendary peak and the highest one in Greece, the previous year. And she regularly thought nothing of doing ten-mile hikes around Kea. Inspired by her walks, we decided we really needed to try one we had never done before. Thus on a windy October late morning, we set out for the Bay of Otzia by way of the old stone footpath, a two hour hike through some of the loveliest areas of the island.

Once you leave the auto roads behind, another Kea opens up before you. Suddenly you have a feel for Kea a hundred years ago or even five hundred years ago. There is the beauty of the landscape, the finding of unexpected farmhouses—some lived in and others abandoned—the plants and wildflowers, the animals, and the feeling of the wind and sun on your face. The island is crisscrossed to this day with dozens of such stone paths, reminders of how busy the island was in the past with a population that was mobile on foot and on donkey or mule.

"Look, Mom!" Caroline called out, finding a calf so young its umbilical cord was still dangling as it nudged its hefty bull dad at one point. And at another we had a view of one of the most perfectly realized stone threshing floors I had ever seen.

We were quite proud to reach the sea still feeling fresh. In fact, the hike had given us renewed energies. So we continued by walking all the way back to the port, looking in on weekend homes built and under construction, olive trees beginning to groan with ready fruit, and once we reached the small yacht port of Vourkari, shops and tavernas closing down for the winter.

Best of all was the chance to get to know Effy better. To hear her tales was worth the hike alone. She knows Kea inside out and gains deep pleasure living here, especially since her home has long since been built and she has no real worries about dealing with the Byzantine give-and-take of being forced to do real business with island workers or contractors.

JOURNEY TO DELPHI AND BEYOND

One weekend in October we decided to go "off the island" and join Judy and Tim for a long weekend journey to Delphi and beyond. Staying on Kea always brings on opposing feelings of "I'm enjoying it here, and I can't bear to leave the island," and "But since we are here we might as well see more, especially so Sam and Caroline will understand Kea is not all of Greece!"

The later argument won out, and by late Friday afternoon we were checking into the Hermes Hotel in Delphi and listening to Sam explaining to Caroline on the balcony how much he had enjoyed Delphi back in June when he had come for a night with my Laughing Out Loud comedy study group.

Judy and Tim showed up shortly afterwards, and we feasted in a fine taverna complete with a hearty local wine and the bracing autumn mountain air.

I can't count the times I've been to Delphi and visited the scene of the ancient Oracle and Apollo's shrine, but it is always a healing experience. Ah, those ancients knew how to choose their sacred spots. From the balcony we could look out over millions of olive trees flowing to the Gulf of Corinth. And off to the left was Mt. Parnassos whose slopes are home to many immortals, rivaled only by Mt. Olympus.

The next morning we rambled happily through the ruins, winding our way up to the stadium for a footrace which Sam won handily with Caroline following up yelling, "Sam, you didn't let me win!"

I looked out over the view from the stadium and pondered: if Delphi was considered the navel of the ancient universe, where had that center shifted to in the modern world? Japan? Wall Street? Moscow? Alas, no oracle or answer came. We moderns have lost such a sense of certainty and security.

We moved up the coast of the mainland after a picnic lunch on the beach at the busy little harbor of Naphpaktos and headed into Epirus, the mountain filled region of northern Greece. Deep ravines, swift rivers, and forests dot sheer mountain ranges. This is definitely a Greece the average tourist looking for sun and sea never encounters. It is the "Other" Greece that has always been fiercely independent, where Greeks and Vlachs who are shepherding people with their own language have shared the slopes and valleys.

There is strength and dignity in such isolation. But for many of those from Epirus, there has been much pain, suffering, loneliness and cruelty. Poverty and the flight abroad of the men and indeed whole families helped depopulate entire mountain villages, and the bloody Greek Civil War of 1945 to 1949 left several hundred more Epirots dead in the hate-filled self slaughtering that took place.

Driving through the lovely yet lonely mountains, I was reminded of the first feature film made by the much awarded Greek director, Theo Angelopoulos, *Reconstruction* (*Anaparastasis*, 1970). Shot in black and white in one of these depopulated villages, it begins with Angelopoulos' own voice over telling us that before World War II, there had been over 3,000 inhabitants, but that by 1966, there were only eighty-five. What follows is a "re-construction" of a true story from a newspaper about a village woman whose husband returns from years of working in Germany and is murdered by his wife and her lover from the village. The mythic pattern, of course, is that of the Agamemnon legend, but what unfolds is really a history of the region in recent years which, if not sympathetically told, at least captures the wife's actions without condemning her. The film launched Angelopoulos' career in 1970 as a kind of shock treatment for Greece to look in the mirror and think about that "other" Greece that had basically been ignored till then.

Epirus today is another matter. Preservationists and conservationists have teamed up to pass various pieces of legislation to preserve wilderness areas and to provide funds for the restoration of many of these villages which have suddenly become trendy escape destinations for Athenians tired of the usual tourist spots on the islands.

And at the center of it all, lies the city of Iannina, pleasantly situated on a tranquil lake. I had been here many years before and had known it as an exotic city with many of the centuries old minarets dotting the skyline as a reminder of the Turkish rule and especially the "independent" fiefdom of the loved and feared Ali Pasha. So I was not prepared for the modern bustling Iannina, complete with a very active university and booming shopping centers giving this city of over a hundred thousand a very European flavor.

Happily, the lakeside section of the city is still full of lake trout and frog legs tavernas and coffee shops. And even more happily, we discovered on a Saturday night that the whole city becomes a very youthful place as teens and college students mix and stroll, laugh and sing.

Sunday morning found us searching for the second most important oracle in Greece after Delphi: Dedoni. Unlike Delphi, Dedoni is quite undiscovered.

Some twenty kilometers out of Iannina and high in the mountains, Dedoni today consists of a huge ancient theater, extensive ruins and several oak trees, which were the source of the prophecies of the past as priests "read" the rustling of the leaves.

We had agreed that we would picnic with the oracle, so before we arrived at the site, I turned up the road to a small mountain village. Underline "small," for this alpine hamlet barely had a road and sported only one *pandopoleon* (general store) which, in the old Greek village tradition, is also a *kafeneon* and small taverna. Several old fellows with long moustaches sat around drinking tsipoura, a powerful homemade brandy, while an elderly couple was behind the counter. Clearly we were the first foreigners in a long, long time (a fact they confirmed), and they insisted I have a shot of *tsipoura* before leaving. Of course shopping for a picnic in such a place wound up yielding a spartan meal of some mean-tasting salami, some fine local cheese and equally tasty local bread. I left with a smile on my face. I have seldom found such a happy small location.

We feasted at Dedoni listening to the breeze blowing through the oak trees. Here was complete calm as Sam and Caroline raced up the steep sides of the ancient theater and performed skits for invisible ancient audiences.

Our final destination was Meteora, several hundred kilometers away. The sun was setting as we approached this unique area, not only for Greece but also of the world. For in an area of only a few square miles are striking rock formations like those in Monument Valley, Utah, but bunched all together here with monasteries and nunneries on the peaks of many of them, representing centuries of holy worship in elevated isolation.

"Wow!" cried out Sam and Caroline. "Can we climb up there?"

"Tomorrow morning," Odette replied.

When I had been there before more than twenty years ago, one could still feel the mystical power of the area. As monks led you through their monasteries, you had to reach after much climbing. And we too in the present all enjoyed the October early morning beauty of Meteora as we sat at the foot of one of the monasteries, waiting for 9 a.m. to ring in so we could enter.

But for me there was a sadness about the present "over selling" of the area. The nearby town has become a cluttered horror of cheaply built but overpriced hotels, junk gift shops and ho-hum tavernas. Meanwhile on the peaks, monasteries have closed over the years, monks have dwindled in numbers to their present numbers of three in one location, five in another and so on. As I stood alone admiring the view from one monastery, I heard laughter and a gossipy monologue with pauses. I looked up to see a monk on the balcony above me sporting sunglasses and chatting away on his cellular phone. Clearly even monastic life is not what it used to be. And as Odette stormed out of a high priced gift shop in one monastery after being badly treated by the employee who was not, of course, a monk, we headed back to Kea eager for our familiar Cycladic calm.

Though we drove through some ugly industrial towns on the way back, we still felt the special moments at Delphi, Dedoni, Iannina, and even in the crisp early morning of Meteora had made it all worthwhile.

"Greece is so much bigger than I thought before," Sam said as we headed into Lavrion, ready for the ferry to Kea.

"I want to go back to Delphi," Caroline added. "Maybe I'll win the race next time!"

SAM FINDS THE TITANIC'S SISTER

"It's so cool," Sam shouted when he caught up with me. "They are diving for the Brittanic, the sister ship of the Titanic! And they said I can see the Jacques Costeau video tomorrow!"

November had just rolled in after we celebrated Halloween on Kea by painting our faces up as goblins, vampires, and the likes. And then Sam made an amazing discovery. We had noticed that the Hotel Karthea in the port was humming with activity with a lot of diving wet suits hanging from balconies.

When Sam, Caroline, and Odette checked it out, they were thrilled to learn that in fact this was a group of about thirty divers, from England mostly. But some were also from Sweden, Canada, and the States and all had gathered, each paying his or her way, to have a crack at diving one hundred forty meters down to do some serious investigating of the Brittanic, the Titanic's sister.

We had actually seen a television documentary earlier in the year in the States about the Brittanic and so already knew that it was larger than the Titanic and had been taken over as a hospital ship for wounded troops. Yet when it was sunk by either German torpedoes or German mines (not mimes!), it was basically empty for it was on a run towards Turkey and thus the Gallipoli area.

Thus over the next week, we all drifted in and out of the hotel, chatting with Poppy, our friend whose family owns the hotel and who was, of course, thrilled to have a full hotel in November. And we spoke with the divers. Not only that, they didn't mind on those evenings we were down in the harbor when we looked over their shoulders in the lobby as they showed the latest videos they had shot that day of the wreckage.

Actually, the divers had a magical effect on Sam and thus on Caroline too. For though early rising had never been a strong point for either of them, they now woke at seven to be down at the harbor, Odette accompanying, to breakfast with the divers, especially

Dave, an English diving instructor, and his wife to catch the latest news.

A FAMILY MEAL AT TASSOS'

Ironically, one of the people I got to know best on Kea was Tassos, who has run OTE, the phone office, for more than twenty years. I often spent a good forty-five minutes each morning doing my e-mail and chatting with him about Kea, his young boys, and more. Thus when he invited us to supper one night, I was very happy to accept, not only because I knew we would enjoy meeting his family, but also because we were literally neighbors since his home was less than seventy-five yards away.

And they gave us a gift. It was a collection of English and American children's songs in English and Greek with Tassos' sons' drawings and those of other classmates within the text too, all collected and turned into a most attractive little book. So Sam and Caroline could then learn "Old MacDonald Had A Farm," "If You're Happy and You Know It, Clap Your Hands," and "I Love Sixpence" in Greek!

CAMPING AT ST. SIMEON

On a blustery Sunday afternoon in November, we set off in the Peugeot to fulfill our promise to have a "family camping trip" on Kea. But we were definitely cutting the corners. Yes, Sam and I had done a real hike and camp out at St. Phillipos a few weeks earlier. This time, however, our actual goal was more modest: to sleep in the guest quarters at the church of St. Simeon on a mountaintop we could reach by car.

That said, it was a perfect experience. The sky was dramatically dark in large part with points of light shining through and illuminating the sea. The whole countryside was definitely greening, and winter wild flowers were in bloom. No more than half an hour after we pulled up to the church and shelter and unloaded, a young fellow showed up in a Nissan pickup truck. He asked if we wanted the key to the other small room attached to the guest dining room we had staked out for the night. He had seen us come up and wanted to offer further hospitality.

As the sun set and Odette and I toasted each other with a hearty red local wine, we once again realized how very real the concept of hospitality was on Kea in a way we had not seen anywhere else in Greece.

The guestroom was equipped with electricity, plates, a burner, benches, tables, and was quite snug once the door was closed. Odette had cooked up a tasty batch of lentils, and together with a winter salad of cabbage, feta, and onion bathed in olive oil, we feasted as the wind beat against the three-foot thick walls.

Before turning in, we all lit candles inside the chapel next door, enjoying the play of light and shadow the candles created on the faces of the saints and Christ on the walls and altar up front. As always, those unanswered questions that fill one's head in Greece. Why St. Simeon, the founder of the Serbian Orthodox church who had become a monk on Mt. Athos hundreds of years ago? No one I asked seemed to know how Serbia and Kea came together or why.

We then placed the benches together to form a sleeping platform. And after the evening's reading of Homer, songs, and stories, we campers were soundly asleep by nine. And as I fell asleep, I felt grateful we were camping safely inside, protected by a Serbian saint in the Cyclades.

STAYING IN TOUCH: E-MAIL REVISITED

We had no phone on Kea. But e-mail did prove to be one continuous embrace of our friends and family and the way to take care of business without going off the island. Thus we knew the latest news from my mother in Florida or exactly when Odette's sister and her husband would fly to China to pick up the adopted child they so wished for or how my former students scattered around the country were doing in Boston and New Orleans and Los Angeles and beyond.

There was also the speedy business side of arranging our journey to and stay in New Zealand, in keeping up with my various book projects with editors in New York and California, and in helping screenwriters who tracked me down from various countries.

Of course Sam and Caroline also kept up with their friends too by e-mail, but this, for the most part, meant Odette wrote the mothers involved. Still, all in all, and subtracting the bothersome mail received along the way too, this new form of communication made our life on a Greek island easier and more enjoyable. So much of what depended on the very uncertain winds of fate if dealing with the Greek post office, was now handled instantly and precisely.

Thus we thanked Hermes, the god of messages for this!

WE PURCHASE OUR FIRST MONASTERY

I want to buy an old Kean monastery, a long unused nunnery named the Monastery of Dafni to be exact. There are, however, two main obstacles: it is not for sale, and I don't have the money for such a purchase.

But in our active imaginations, Odette and I purchased our first monastery while on Kea.

Why buy a nunnery, you ask? Simple. In all the years Odette and I have come to Kea, we had never noticed this particular location, tucked away almost out of sight of the paved road leading to the upper road above the village and beyond towards the central and lower parts of the island. But in reading a recent guidebook to the island, we came across a striking photo of the old holy spot, and on a blustery October afternoon, I set out on a jogging hike (jogging on pavement, hiking on stone paths) to find it. Which I did. But I was taking it in from a distance since the monastery and the surrounding hillside were fenced off as the private property it has become.

I was struck immediately with that realization of, "Yes, this is the one place on this island that I would sell my soul to own!" And all ideas of renouncing private property, which I had ever entertained, especially as influenced by Tolstoy's later life and writings, immediately evaporated! For before me was a gorgeous hill sticking up from the mountain slope, tree shaded and sporting the old buildings of a small walled in monastery which would, at its peak, have housed no more than a dozen nuns. I could make out the church in the center of this holy cluster and the several surrounding buildings, which would have been the dorm rooms, kitchen and storerooms. The guidebook made it clear it had been bought by one of the most respected families on the island, but local word of mouth had it that the actual relatives who presently owned it lived out of the country and almost never used it.

I jogged home with fantasies of how Odette and Sam and Caroline and I could transform the place into a home for friends, students, and screenwriters looking for inspiration. The following day we brazenly parked the car at the top of the private road, opened the gate, and hiked down the two hundred meters to the monastery. We were not disappointed. The present owners had maintained the pleasing simplicity and beauty of the location, and through the windows that were not blocked, we could see that all had been kept in utter simplicity with no fancy renovations other than the addition of electricity and some plumbing.

As is usual still on Kea, the church was unlocked. I lit my prayer candle after paying for mine and Sam and Caroline's. Then I said a quiet prayer to myself. "Of course I will never own this holy and beautiful spot, but I ask forgiveness if from time to time I drop by to savor the peace and inspiration this monastery inspires."

So far my prayers have been answered!

WHEN NEW ORLEANS COMES TO KEA

We had a special treat our last week on the island. One of our best friends from New Orleans, Andrew MacDonald, came to visit.

He too was a professor at Loyola University in New Orleans on sabbatical and was savoring the last two months of freedom before returning to the classroom. A large fellow from Texas, he possessed a hearty laugh, a twinkle in his eye, and a solid beard. Andrew hopped on an inexpensive Delta standby flight and arrived at Athens Airport on an almost balmy morning in November.

"At long last we see you again in person rather than on e-mail!" I said, leading him towards the Peugeot.

Andrew and his wife Gina, also a professor at Loyola but with a part time status, had helped us in so many ways, including caring for our beloved cat, Laura, who had been incorporated into their family of fourteen other cats. They had also been good at checking mail and faxes and messages from Loyola and staying on top of e-mail updates to us so we would know the good, the bad, and the ugly of campus and departmental politics.

"Gina sends greetings and is jealous she has to teach instead of joining me in Greece with you all," Andrew said an hour later, sipping strong Greek coffee at the café beside the temple of Poseidon at Cape Sounion, the whole Aegean spread out before him.

And thus began a festive last week on Kea as I checked Andrew into Hotel Karthea amidst the bustle of the Brittanic divers coming and going. Odette had a tasty hot supper for us that night. The wine flowed and Andrew's jet lag began to melt away with news of home and work, the latest outrages in New Orleans, and the progress of the numerous book projects he and his wife had underway both together and separately.

Andrew had hurt one leg doing some carpentry on a house they owned in Austin, Texas, so negotiating the hundred odd steps up to our home took some maneuvering. But over the next few days, he began to become the half-goat, half-human person that all Keans must be to negotiate the streets, paths, and byways of the island.

And we managed to cram a lot in with Andrew in our final days, including a plunge into the sea for a brief swim—the last of the journey for me and his only Greek sea adventure—at Otzia Beach on the way to the monastery.

Odette and I were touched by his friendship and his joyous outreaches to join us given the time, distance, and finances involved. His visit made it all the more clear to us how important our time together on the island but apart from our regular routine and environment had been in so many ways. Including that of savoring friendships all the more over distance and, in the case of Andrew, through a sharing of the experience itself.

There was much laughter that week. But Andrew was also a friendly yet very real reminder of the changes we were embracing as a family. For as the Kea experience unfolded, we were beginning to officially withdraw from New Orleans as our Oklahoma future became more clear. Odette handled the complexities of buying a house by phone, fax, and Greek Fed Ex, quite successfully as it turned out. And I stayed busy on e-mail, checking on the progress of my candidacy for the offer of the position at Oklahoma to become an approved tenured slot.

By the time Andrew arrived, all of these wheels of fate and fortune had turned and made Oklahoma our new home at the end of our year long journey, for sure with a final complete job contract promised by the end of January.

The emotional ties and friendships for us and Sam and Caroline were, of course, another matter. Having Andrew with us that last week meant a lot as we weathered all of these feelings plus the very real pains of leaving the island we loved.

The highlight of his visit, however, was, it turned out, our overnight stay with Vasso and Argiris at Petrousa, Argiris' family home at the southern end of the island. It is a huge stretch of mountainous land reaching to the sea with a simple farmhouse that Argiris and his brother Kostas were born and raised in and which to this day still had no running water or electricity. Next to the original farmhouse was the "new" home—a large one room affair that was a bedroom for three or more, a dining room, living room and kitchen all in one, which Argiris had built over the past ten years.

The trip to Petrousa had become the crowning highlight of previous visits to the island for us. But it was not just the simplicity of the life there that was the attraction or even the splendid view of the sea and the island of Kythnos beyond it. Rather, it was the chance to see Kostas again. Kostas is a few years older than Argiris and is, since early childhood, deaf and mute. Put simply, we all love him and have done so all the years we have been privileged to know him.

KOSTAS SPEAKS

"They came again!"

"Brother and Vasso signaled me that they would come and showed me a new photo that I like very much. The little girl has such bright eyes and the boy has a big smile, like mine. They make me happy! I mean, almost nobody comes here and of course, NEVER to spend the night as this American family does, sleeping in the new house.

"But they didn't come in the Toyota with Brother, and I was confused till Vasso signaled that they had a car. And then before they arrived I had time to check on some of the sheep I had not seen for two days.

"Vasso had already put out all of the food for this Sunday visit but there was of course a lot more this week since the Americans were coming and bringing a friend, and then they were here! A big shinny car and the little girl came up and gave me a hug, and I hugged the boy too and embraced the man and his wife and shook hands with their friend, a big man with a beard. He looked like he could do farm work too, but Brother signaled he was a teacher too like the American, Andreas. And Vasso signaled that the friend was also named Andreas and I thought that was very funny—two friends named Andreas!

"Oh, I was excited! I brought the girl and the boy over to the yard and showed them Bayam, my dog, and I showed them lots of things. I showed them some funny shells I found down on the beach and all the dead wasps, which had been eating the old grapes, I had caught. Ah, I like to see the children here!

"So we ate the mountain of food Vasso had prepared and I kept filling the wineglasses too!

"It was such a good day that I almost forgot about the HORROR, but I can never forget about it, so after some more wine, I begin signaling Brother again about it. Because I wanted the two Andreas fellows to know too, I signaled how I was walking down near the beach by the old mine and I found one of our sheep, murdered, stripped, and tossed on the beach. Then I found another and another and another.

"And I went crazy. What had happened? How could anybody kill our sheep? Who were they? Where did they come from? WHY? WHY? WHY?

"I signaled that God would punish them for God is good. Those men came to our land and killed our sheep, and took away the meat, for that was the reason. And when I calmed down just a bit, I could see they came by boat, did their dirty work and left.

"I felt HORRIBLE. The worst I have felt in my life. Bad enough to live alone unable to talk or hear, all these years. But then THIS. And what if they did it because they knew I couldn't hear. That makes me even more crazy. But I've had too much wine now, because I start to think like those cowboy movies I've seen at Brother's house on the television, that maybe if Brother and I and the two Andreas professors all go together, we will find those bad guys and that will be that! But the little American girl smiles and I laugh and my troubles go away.

"Yet I get sad inside, because I know they will leave and I will be alone again. Never mind for now. They are here and I am happy."

LANDSCAPE IN THE MIST: FAREWELL TO KEA

We left Kea at dawn on a chilly November morning with mist pouring in over the harbor. "I don't want to leave," said Caroline, standing on the deck looking out at the port fading away in the mist. And I knew what she meant. Andrew and I sipped hot metreo coffees as Kea was slowly enveloped in fog. I felt that sharp pain deep inside that I recognized from other journeys that ended, other departures from Kea.

This time the twinge was even more intense. For we as a family and as individuals had been very happy on the island. We had shared so many good times, friends, and quiet moments too. Wherever else we were headed would be "different" and apart from the encircled security of our island life. "When will we return?" Odette wondered aloud. I had no easy answer. Too much was uncertain.

Our last evening had been shared with Stephanos and Katerina, first over wine in our home and then at Yiannis' taverna in the square. What was special about the gathering was that it seemed so ordinary: just another fine meal shared with good friends. There was one ironic difference, however: the television was blaring as usual, but this time the images were those of an American television version of Homer's Odyssey starring Armand Assante as Odysseus. We had seen this tele-epic in the States before coming to Europe. That meant before Sam and Caroline had HEARD Homer as well. Thus while I was amused at the Greek subtitles as this English speaking Odysseus confronted an English speaking Cyclops, Caroline added only one comment after several moments of viewing time: "It's not as good as Homer!"

Odette and I smiled and winked. All of those evenings reading The Odyssey had not been lost upon Sam and Caroline.

But the pain of departure lasted only briefly, for we were swiftly caught up in the strange magic of the thick fog that surrounded us. We had never seen anything like it. Nothing existed beyond a few feet in front of our eyes. Then Sam came running, saying, "We're not moving. We should be landing now. What's happening?"

And he was right. What we learned was that the Lavrion harbor master would not let us land. So we sat, motionless, suspended in time and space, waiting. It was a strange experience to say the least. An hour later, however, once we did finally disembark, we were soon driving up a clear coastline towards Athens with the fog far behind us.

That was not to be our last memory of leaving Kea. For that evening as we were going out from the Hotel Aphrodite for a feast with Judy, Tim, and Judy's daughter Ierene, and friends from the University of Oklahoma, we learned that a Lithuanian ship had collided in the mist with a Syrian tanker, and five sailors had drowned. The news for days was full of the collision near Kea. "I can't believe the boat sank almost at the exact spot where the Brittanic sank," Sam added.

We had many more voyages to enjoy ahead of us. But this tragic collision in the mist was an ancient reminder that not all journeys end safely or happily. Five unlucky men would never reach Ithaca.

LAKIS COMES THROUGH

Lakis smiled and took another mouthful. "Ah, Odette, your gumbo is even better than the one you made last year in New Orleans!" There was loud agreement from all around the table as farewell toasts to us were offered. I was especially happy. My friend Lakis whom I had only barely seen once while in Greece this trip, had come through. He was to be the friend who came to our last supper in Athens.

Our final night in Athens was spent with our friends Katerina and Vlasis in Katerina's spacious home. We had come full circle, for this is where we had arrived that rainy midnight back in September. There could be no better way to leave Athens. And to make it even better, Odette had asked if we could cook up a gumbo instead of going out to yet another taverna. After all, we loved the warmth of Katerina's house, which reflects her spirit and laughter. Thus she, remembering her evenings in New Orleans was enthusiastic about our offer, and so the shopping began for a closing feast.

We were happy but also very tired. There had been more meals with other friends, last minute shopping in Plaka and then the move from the hotel to Katerina's home.

I, on the other hand, was pleased to, at long last, see my friend Lakis Lazopoulos, who happens to be the funniest man alive in Greece. Lakis is something of a Jerry Seinfeld and Robin Williams rolled into one body and spirit. For four years he had the most popular Greek television show ever. He played roughly fourteen different characters he had created, written, produced and directed each week, and almost everyone in Greece still quotes lines, remembers scenes, and argues passionately over their favorites of the many characters ranging from a snooty uptown old socialite or a ditsy blond gal to a crazed cab driver and a neurotic television anchor man.

During the previous year, he and I had written a feature comedy, and he was eager to get the film, his first effort at cinema, off the ground in the near future. I had never had more fun writing a script, and the time we spent together working on the project both in New Orleans and Athens had turned us into kindred comic souls and good friends. But while I had been enjoying the peace and tranquility of Kea, he had been living his usual frenetic life in Athens. He had wanted to come and relax with us, but as the director of a theater where one of his plays about to go on, with a television special he had just completed, and an Australian film project also under way, he could never break away. Even to join us on what was our final evening, he had driven directly from the main television studio where he had been interviewed on the evening news about the cultural politics in Greece at that moment. As Sam, one of his biggest fans, put it, "Wow, it's pretty amazing to watch him on television and then have him ring the doorbell fifteen minutes later!"

Andrew was there enjoying the festivities as well before heading back to New Orleans, and our friends Penny and Costas also stopped by. The wine and laughter and even some heated discussion of current issues filled the Athenian evening

"To comedy and gumbo and friendship," toasted Lakis as the spirited evening came to a close. And as we left Athens behind the next morning.

TRAGEDY ON CEPHALONIA

Before leaving Greece, we had to visit two islands that we had never been to before: Cephalonia and Ithaca. From Athens, the toll road to the port city of Patras is a surprisingly swift road. And after an afternoon spent looking around Patras, the third largest city in Greece, a center for much of the Greek wine industry and a community well known for its long tradition of carnival, we were on a ferry for the large island of Cephalonia.

With roughly 40,000 residents, Cephalonia is certainly one of Greece's largest islands, and with its forests and mountains, it is a beautiful one quite different in appearance from the unforested Cycladic islands. The island had been almost totally destroyed by earthquakes in the 1950s. And so there is an unusual mixture of recent architecture and crumbling ruins that were simply abandoned. We spent a night in the lively capital city of Sami and read that night the scene from *The Odyssey* in which Odysseus and Telemachus finally meet up, and Odysseus reveals his identity. "I am not a god. I am your father," he says, and we found ourselves—all of us—crying. Homer has that power!

But we had even more tears in our eyes the next day. For we visited the Italian memorial outside of Sami to the Italian soldiers stationed on Cephalonia in World War II who were slaughtered by their allies, the Nazis, for becoming too friendly to the Greeks. The memorial says it is dedicated to the 5,000 men who were simply executed by the Germans, the additional 3,500 who were drowned by them, and the 1,500 who died resisting execution. 10,000 men in arms whose crime was that they began to question what the war was all about. Sam put it best: "War is stupid, Dad." What to say? "You are right, son. You are so right. If only nations would listen to you, to us!"

That day we drove through stunning countryside, visiting the charming fishing village of Friskardo, the enchanting mountain village of Tsilendara where our friend Penny's family on her father's side came from and after whom the village, Tsilentis, is named, and then down the coast where we spent the night.

We slept well, but I had images of earthquakes, of the Italians, and of Homer's *Odyssey* mixing in my mind as well. Odette put it well too that these quiet times together as a family again were important. This was, after all, a kind of transition from our time on Kea and our moments with friends in Athens, before we left this country we love so much and continued our own odyssey through Europe towards home.

"I don't want to leave Greece," said Caroline, already preparing herself for yet another departure. I gave her a hug. "We will be back," I said. "I know," she said. "But I still don't want to leave."

Lights out and the sound of the winter winds beginning to blow against the coastline outside.

ITHACA AT LAST:
A SECOND CONVERSATION WITH HOMER

We had reached Ithaca at last and had begun with great excitement to explore this legendary island where Odysseus supposedly lived and ruled. At one point I was changing some dollars in a travel agency in Vathi, the port and capital of the island.

When the young man at the desk found out where we were from after the obligatory Greek, *Apo pou eistei?* (Where are you from?), he immediately reached over to his crowded stack of CDs, pulled out one, and slapped it into his Sony player. Louis Armstrong singing "Hello, Dolly" began to fill the room and, indeed, the harbor beyond. Sam, Caroline, and Odette smiled.

Once outside, we strolled by the pleasant waterfront filled with echoes of The Odyssey. There was the Penelope Grill, and the Odysseus Hotel where we had already checked in, thanks to the Albanian cleaning woman who was mopping the floors. Further along was a butcher shop named Eumaeus, after Odysseus' swineherd, and there was even a Cyclops Bar. But as we had almost reached our car and were walking past the Odyssey kafeneon, I heard a strangely familiar, "Hello."

I turned to see "him" again, sitting with several local youths in sunglasses, tight jeans and leather jackets and with nearly shaved heads.

"Homer, don't tell me you are here too?"

He gestured us to sit and chuckled, "Well, my boy, this is my man Odysseus' island after all!"

Odette, Sam, and Caroline were completely speechless at first.

"We love your stories," said Caroline, sitting next to the Bard.

She was proud that she managed this in Greek, thanks to Katerina's lessons, and Homer complimented her on her achievement. "We have been seeing Odysseus' houses," Sam added in Greek with obvious pride and then turned to me to ask Homer if Odysseus was a real person.

Homer laughed and sipped his metreo coffee being careful not to spill it on his toga. "Real is a difficult word and concept, isn't it?" he asked. "You must remember the Trojan War took place hundreds of years before I was born, so I never met the man himself."

Eumaius, the butcher, walked by and called out a greeting.

"Ithaca is beautiful, but some people say Odysseus lived on the island of Lefkas or Cephalonia next door," said Odette in her newly acquired Greek. Homer smiled and sighed. "Ah, those scholars give me a royal pain in my...," he said as he cleared his throat. "But does it really matter? What I clearly mean is that he is from the Ionian isles and the Ionian Sea. Odysseus was not from the Cyclades and the Aegean Sea where you all were spending time on Kea! That seems to me the point."

By then the two young islanders took their leave and we moved closer to the Bard as he finished his coffee. "We have already been to the Cave of the Nymphs where Odysseus stored his treasures once he landed back on Ithaca," I added. "And also the site that the British and German archeologists first thought was Odysseus' palace, but which they now believe was just another ancient Mycenian town."

Homer was leaning on his staff, and brushed aside my comments with a sweep of his hand. "I have a more simple question for you. Isn't Ithaca beautiful and peaceful?"

"Absolutely," I added as my metreo arrived.

"And I love seeing the people gathering the olives," Odette said. "There was even a fellow riding his motorcycle as the sun set carrying his olive ladder as he drove along."

"Ah, motorcycles and olives," the Bard sighed. "But I also enjoy this modern town for Vathi is very special. Have you noticed anything unusual here?"

He was testing me now and I was enjoying it.

"Well, I've never seen another island with a road sign like the one over there pointing to THE CULTURAL CENTER, THE CINEMA, and THE LIBRARY."

"Exactly!" said Homer giving Caroline a hug. "This is an island with a high level of culture and education due to the strong influence of a very active left wing political movement."

Then I commented, "The fellow who sold me our boat ticket for Patras this morning said he was also the projectionist at the cinema and that they had had a full house at the screening of *The English Patient* last night."

"Yes, I know, I was there!" Homer said with clear enthusiasm.

"You go to the movies?" Sam questioned. "Wow! But your ... eyes."

"I like to hear the dialogue and music and the audience reactions," Homer replied. "Last week it was a new Woody Allen film and all the young people got the jokes. It was marvelous."

By then he was standing to leave. "May I have an autograph?" Sam quickly got out. "I have a collection and got Shaquille O'Neil's this summer," he continued. Homer laughed. "I don't know how to write!" he said, patting Sam on his shoulders.

Odette whispered in my ear and then I asked the Bard a final question. "Is there any final meaning you want us to get from your wonderful poems?" I asked. Homer shook his head playfully. "I'm a story teller and a poet, not a philosopher or a priest!" he said. "Excuse me, but I must be off, young man, and happy travels to the whole family."

"Thank you, but I really don't feel I'm that young anymore."

"But in comparison to ME?" came back the Bard with a hearty laugh.

And he was off, whistling "Hello Dolly" quietly as he faded away.

That evening, our last in Greece, we stopped by the cinema before the projection on the invitation of the projectionist I had met earlier that day. He was proud of the old giant arc light projector that one never sees anymore in the States. It was a beauty. I asked for his name and address so I could send the film club some of my books since I was impressed with the kinds of activities the club sponsored in the name of their love of cinema.

Later that night before turning in at the Hotel Odysseus, I looked at the paper he gave me and his name really was: Homer!

TRANSITIONS:
CHRISTMAS IN AMERICA

Leaving Greece meant travels through Italy, Switzerland where I taught screenwriting for two weeks in beautiful Montreux at the International Academy of Broadcasting, and then on to some of Odette's relatives in Germany, and finally back to Paris to leave our trusty Peugeot and to England to revisit old friends before heading back to America for Christmas.

MISSING EUROPE ALREADY: TAKING STOCK

Gatwick Airport early on a cold December morning. We had sped by taxi through dark streets with ease and began checking in our mountain of luggage at the Delta desk upon arrival. At Passport Control, the friendly flush faced official looked at Caroline in her 101 Dalmatians-spotted jacket and wryly asked, "What happened to the other 100, mate?"

Caroline laughed and then announced with a tear as we were climbing on the plane, "I don't want to leave … Europe." We all felt that pang: Europe collectively was now the combined term for all of the departures we had been going through since leaving Kea over three weeks before.

Once buckled in, however, I asked Sam and Caroline a question as the beginning of our process of taking stock of their whole experience. Question: "if you could go back to five places we have visited in Europe, NOT COUNTING KEA, which is a given as a kind of second home, where would you go?" Both of them took to the question immediately and began thinking and writing. The lists were:

CAROLINE	SAM
1. Montreux, Switzerland	1. Montreux
2. The Cotswolds, England	2. Lake Ochrid, Macedonia
3. Ithaca, Greece	3. The Cotswolds
4. Macedonia	4. Ithaca
5. Slovenia	5. Budapest, Hungary

Soon the routine of meals and films took over on the flight and their attentions went elsewhere. But in my mind a flood of images and memories kept coming back. It had been a wonderful adventure, and Odette and I kissed good luck that no major disasters had occurred. And I thought to myself how blessed we had been with friends and opportunities on this journey, filling us with memories that were now a part of who we were. These were not guaranteed from the beginning, and I am speaking mainly from Sam and Caroline's perspectives.

Before falling into a long winter's nap, I thought of a number of "what ifs" in that light. What if Sam and Caroline had not gotten on well together, or what if one or the other or both had such an overly strong case of home sickness, including missing their friends, that the pleasure of travel or even travel itself would have had to been altered or terminated? But none of these had been our experience. For we had lived fully abroad as a family and as each of our own selves as well.

NEW ORLEANS AT CHRISTMAS

White Christmas lights tastefully done in elaborate designs on the mansions of St. Charles Avenue are part of the fun of the Christmas season in New Orleans. Andrew and Gina MacDonald met us at the airport, and while we spoke with great animation about our shared experiences on Kea with Andrew, we were enjoying our homecoming once more even though we were very aware we had no house to return to. But our friends Rayza and Claudio welcomed us into their spacious and beautiful Uptown home near Audibon Park, and we all slept feeling the comfort of a city and friends we knew well.

In the next few days, we all enjoyed the pleasures of the season, seeing friends, catching up on news, and for me, running into students and colleagues and hearing what they had been up to as well. Somehow our return had not been as difficult as I perhaps had imagined it. Our travels and experiences abroad had been part of an on-going process of letting go of New Orleans as our "home town." It was now the familiar city where a lot of friends lived and where memories of our years here came back to us from time to time. This new feeling was not unpleasant, and Sam and Caroline were too busy with the pleasure of seeing their friends for any sadness to seep in. Likewise for Odette. Our list of things we needed to get done, on top of seeing friends and family, meant she was quite focused and on the move during our brief Christmas stay.

CHRISTMAS IN FLORIDA

Mom whipped up a feast, seemingly without effort, that first evening in Atlantic Beach, Florida. We had driven in from New Orleans, arriving after lunch and had already settled Sam and Caroline down the road even closer to the beach at my sister Suzi's home. "Andy, if you can help take people's drink orders," said Mom as she and Odette brought out several more dishes for the table.

Suddenly we felt Christmas had really begun. Anne, my mother, looked great, and obviously her move to Florida two years before had been good for her. She had a pleasant small two bedroom house less than a mile from the Atlantic ocean in the easy going community of Atlantic Beach some twenty miles from Jacksonville.

I had remembered coming out by myself for a few days before we took off for Europe. At that time I had enjoyed seeing my mother's happy schedule of water aerobics, book groups, Unitarian Church activities, sharing a Saturday morning breakfast group at a sea front hotel with a bunch of characters, and meeting several of her very good new friends. She was thriving on all this. Plus she was living close to my sister Suzi, her husband Jeff, and their eight-year-old son, Matt.

Just then my sister, her family, and Sam and Caroline entered Mom's front door, and the first of many shared seasonal feasts began. Candle light and a welcoming blessing and the laughter and fellowship started up.

PHIL ARRIVES

Phil, my then twenty-three-year-old son, arrived several days later. Mom insisted on picking him up so that she would have the return ride to get a head start on catching up on all his news. It was to be his first Florida visit since "Annie" had moved from Virginia, and Sam and Caroline too were excited about seeing their big brother. We had last met up in May some seven months earlier at his Fordham University graduation in New York and then a week in New Orleans before Sam and I left for the Comedy Seminar in Greece.

A big hug, and he was among us. Smiling, shorter hair for his role of Lysander in Shakespeare's *A Midsummer Night's Dream*, tall and trim.

The next few days were a blur of family, Christmas activity, food, food, and more food, new faces, and walks on the beach. But in the midst of all, Phil managed to balance somehow the time he needed to practice his Shakespeare and yet connect with his brother and sister, grandmother, aunt and uncle by marriage, and cousin. It was not easy, of course, but he showed amazing good will in dealing with being at the center of attention.

That left, of course, remarkably little time for the two of us to spend time together. But moments caught between this and that established contact, and we agreed time alone together each year some way or another would always be a priority. We had had some good times together in Louisiana, but as he spoke of his MFA in the drama program at Carnigie Mellon University and his upcoming semester in Moscow at the famous Art Theatre that produced Chekov and many others, my mind was filled with memories of camping trips with him in Virginia when he was much younger, together with travels through Yugoslavia, including Sarajevo, time in Greece, a week in Los Angeles, a road trip across America, and numerous trips I had made to see him in New York. These and other memories came back fondly.

Then with Odette, Sam, and Caroline, we were packed in the car for an overnight at Disney World some three hours down the road. That too, as our many miles of travel had proved, was a good time for talk.

None of us had ever been to Disney World. But somehow it seemed appropriate that before we four left for New Zealand and Phil for Russia, we should visit the New Jerusalem of pop culture. Sam, Phil, and I had, at differing times, been to Disneyland, and, ironically, it had been my friend Sam in Los Angeles who had taken them. No, we weren't allowed in to Disney World when we arrived at two in the afternoon. "We stopped letting people in at 10:20, Sir," said a parking attendant, "try real early tomorrow."

And so we did after a relaxed afternoon and a steak supper, with Phil sleeping in one motel room with Sam and Caroline, and Odette and I in the other hearing endless giggles from the other room till late that night.

Then we were up by six the next morning. We drove the ten miles to the main entrance, and on an unusually chilly Florida December morning, we were actually some of the first through the gates when they swung open and so we found no wait in line, for the big rides for the first couple of hours anyway, including Splash Mountain, the space ride, and others.

No need to ask what Sam and Caroline thought. And Phil was right in there with them, suddenly a kid again himself, going on some rides with Sam that Odette, Caroline, and I opted out of.

Of course by early afternoon the lines were hours long, the languages spoken were varied, and we were ready to leave after the big Christmas parade. We left just in time for my tastes so that the crushing strangeness of a world where you pay to have mechanical dreams happen to you as you push and shove your way through thousands of others in search of the same pay-and-deliver fix. That's an unfair evaluation for children, of course, yet Disney's Florida "World" seemed an uneasy universe away from the real pleasures of America and Europe we had been experiencing over the past six months. And I thought of my numerous New Orleans students who reported they and friends had spent honeymoons at Disney World. My mind boggled. With a smile, I've often wondered, has anyone done any follow up research on what happens to marriages that start off with Mickey, that major image of the 20th century more recognized than Elvis, Chaplin, Marilyn Monroe, Christ, Hitler, or Bill Clinton.

Never mind for the moment. The Christmas season was still upon us and we had two more days with Phil. Sleepy Disney World survivors meant he and I had more time to talk on the drive back to Atlantic Beach. "Ready for Moscow?" I asked after giving him a number of names, addresses, and fax and phone numbers for my friends in Moscow and St Petersburg. "I'm beginning to get excited, and it's all happening so fast," Phil said. As one retirement center and golf course after another sailed by, we spoke of things Russian, dramatic and, upon return, theatrical and cinematic for a young actor about to make his way in the world of stage, film, and television.

NEW ZEALAND BEGINS IN NEW ORLEANS

Back in New Orleans, we had less than two weeks to prepare for the final part of our year on the road: New Zealand. Of course, we were still very much "in the middle" of seeing old friends each evening and digesting our European experiences. And yet New Zealand began to excite us as we set up a temporary home in a comfortable two bedroom apartment belonging to a Loyola professor in political science and his wife, who were on sabbatical in Europe.

The five months in Wellington, the capital, were to be a faculty exchange with a film studies professor, Harriet, from Victoria University. The whole idea had begun two years before when

Odette and I had visited New Zealand for the first time and had enjoyed it so much we promised we would return with the children.

Thus after many letters, faxes, and e-mails, it was happening: Harriet was to arrive on January 7 so we could meet her and settle her in, and we would take off on the twelth. And so it happened. Thankfully, Harriet had been to New Orleans several times before and was, in fact, an American citizen who had been in New Zealand now for four years. Of course when we originally dreamed up the exchange, we had no idea of leaving New Orleans afterwards. Thus she was to get our home, and we hers. In actuality, the present situation was a better one for her in many ways, since the "sabbatical apartment" was much closer to the Loyola campus than our old home and, frankly, in a safer neighborhood. She still was to get our car, and we would take over her house and car in Wellington.

Jobwise, it was simple: she would teach two film classes at Loyola, and I would likewise teach two at Victoria. Paychecks? No problem, once more. I kept mine and she kept hers.

"Welcome back!" I said as Harriet arrived after the jet lag of all jet lag flights: Wellington to Auckland, Auckland to Los Angeles and Los Angeles to New Orleans." Harriet, trim, smiling, in her 40s, had made it safely. "Wow," she said with surprise as we headed for our car, "Same temperature here and this is summer in Wellington remember!"

Our double new odyssey had begun. We briefed each other over the next few days as we also introduced her to friends. Suddenly, we were excited once more. A new world awaited at the other end of the earth.

MY KIWI FRIEND, CHARLES

"Happy birthday, Charles!" I said, digging into a delicious slice of cake at 10 a.m. one bright January morning in New Orleans before we left.

I was visiting Charles, my New Zealand friend in New Orleans, and, in fact, one of my best friends over the past five years. "It's a bit early, but then we won't see each other till next month in Wellington," said Charles pouring some coffee as Gina, his partner from the New Orleans area (New Zealand term for "significant other"), passed out birthday hats for us to wear in festive celebration.

Charles, from Wellington, is a retired cardiologist who studied medicine in the States, taught for a while at Columbia University, and then ran his own cardiology clinic for years in New Orleans. We met up because of a mutual love of film. I had started and run the New Orleans Film Festival for the first three years of its existence, and we met through various functions connected to the festival. The rest is history: good times shared in New Orleans at films, over meals, and travelling to festivals together, including Sundance and Toronto. And he had joined me on one of my script seminars in Greece. So he qualified as a "Kea alumnus" too!

"You know you are the guilty party here, Charles," I said as sunlight poured into his 12th floor apartment near the harbor at West End on Lake Ponchetrain with a view of the lake and of all of New Orleans.

"Guilty of what?" asked Charles.

"Guilty of getting Odette and me hooked on New Zealand. None of this would be happening if we had not met you." He laughed and we both agreed.

For it was true. We had heard so many wonderful stories of New Zealand over the years, seen photos of his amazing recently purchased farm, his newly built home there, and we had met many of his friends as they came to New Orleans from time to time to visit. Odette and I had a comfortable feeling about the country long before we set foot there two years ago on a brief two-week visit.

"More coffee?" asked Gina, as I took out pen and paper and began to quiz Charles on last minute advice about everything from what spots he would recommend for us to visit, and what we should not forget to bring.

We would be living in Wellington, a windy city of about 300,000 at the far south end of the North Island. The basic facts, we already knew. For instance, our previous trip had made it clear that two thirds of New Zealand's three and a half million people live on the North island, leaving the larger South Island wonderfully under inhabited. And we needed Charles' input, for we were aware that free time for travel would be limited once Sam and Caroline were in school and I was back in the classroom at the Victoria University.

Charles was full of good ideas and radiated enthusiasm even though I knew he was feeling worried and was probably in a good deal of pain. He was facing a hip replacement operation the next week and would have to recover for about six weeks before coming to Wellington and his farm.

"Give my love to Joy and all my other friends when you see them," Charles said as we hugged goodbye. "A speedy recovery and next month in Wellington," I said. "And a safe flight over," added Gina as I left.

HAPPY BIRTHDAY, CAROLINE!

"Make a wish, Caroline, and BLOW!" said Odette, as Caroline, surrounded by five of her girlfriends was celebrating her eighth birthday. It was an unusually balmy Saturday morning in mid January in New Orleans' spacious City Park, and we were set up under huge oak trees in the picnic table area next to Storyland, a satisfyingly simple fantasy play area for children.

A happy occasion by any measure. The girls were catching their breath as the cake was cut since Storyland for them had been Fifteen-different-ways-to-slide down the slide shaped like a friendly dragon. But that was not all. Sam had four of his friends too, and they were off at another picnic table holding their own party though they did yell over birthday greetings to Caroline too.

The energy level and amount of laughter was very high that morning. For while Sam and Caroline had been visiting and, in several cases, spending nights at different friend's homes, there was something very poignant and special about so many friends for each gathered in one space, outdoors, briefly, after so many travels and before we boarded a plane for the other side of the world.

Caroline and her mates were joyfully busy with gift giving and unwrapping while I watched Sam and his friends, three of whom are African-American, talking about music, cars, sports and school. Both Sam and Caroline had gone back to their school, Audibon Montessori, for a day, and Caroline for several days. And it had been a much easier experience than either Odette or I had anticipated.

Then parents arrived, good byes in the park were said, and we were back to packing for New Zealand.

PART TWO: NEW ZEALAND
THE LAND OF THE LONG WHITE CLOUD
SUMMER

"IHI"
"Maori word for quality of excellence. Everything, including animals and plants, has a special power or unique power known as 'ihi.' It is the power of living things to grow and develop to their full maturity and state of excellence."

Cleve Barlow, *Tikanga Whakaaro*

"I have always loved long journeys."

Witi Ihimaera, *Nights in the Gardens of Spain*

MEMORIES OF AOTEAROA

"No problem. It's all in. Do you have any other bags?" asked Kevin Rabalais.

My former student met us on a drizzle filled January afternoon in New Orleans with his trusty pickup and helped me load in our mountain of suitcases and bags for the airport. For Europe we had packed lighter, knowing we would have to cart it all through Europe as we drove. But New Zealand was to be a different story. For this journey, we had only to get to the airport and then from the Wellington Airport to Harriet's house on Moir Street. And unload for five months.

Odette and Caroline drove the rental car and returned it, meeting us at the United Airlines counter. The drive to the airport had been a chance to catch up with Kevin since his visit to Switzerland with us and hear his plans for his last semester before graduation. He also had an exciting project he and his friend Jennifer were embarked on to do a book of interviews with various novelists.

Then we Hortons were a flying team again. New Orleans to LAX, Los Angeles, and, after a delay and phone calls to LA friends, including Harriet and Sam and others, we were off to Aotearoa, the land of the long white cloud, as the Maoris named it when they arrived there over a thousand years ago.

"Hey! A three movie flight, Mom!" Caroline and Sam were amazed. As seasoned travelers to Europe, this concept of a four-teen-hour non-stop flight was new. And they did manage to catch about two and a half films with sleep claiming them for several hours.

I, on the other hand, drifted off after the evening meal with memories of Odette and my two week visit to New Zealand of the past resurfacing happily.

In short, we both fell in love with this country at the other end of the world. But that journey had even more meaning for us since Odette up till that point had never been away from Sam and Caroline for more than two nights at a time. On the decision that it would be good for us as a couple and healthy for them as children for us to have some time alone together each year, we jumped when Air New Zealand offered a buy-one-ticket-and-bring-a-partner-for-$499!

That year Odette and I arrived in Christchurch on the South Island via Auckland and Los Angeles from New Orleans. After seeing friends for lunch, we picked up a rental car. Before giving us the keys, however, the Kiwi agent made us watch a ten-minute video about driving on the left-hand side of the road. "Lots of Yanks get in accidents over here!" he said cheerfully. Then it was the open road through unspoiled coastline, and, as we turned inland, snow-capped mountains with forests leading up their slopes as far as we could see. And sheep. Millions of sheep and almost no people. I'm from Virginia, and I had a very pleasant yet strange sense of deja vu in New Zealand. This was like the Blue Ridge Mountains meets the Alps with a touch of Colorado and Norway thrown in for good measure. We were totally jetlagged but as the sun was sinking we had reached our first night's destination: Hamner Springs, a small mountain resort spa and town with naturally hot springs.

Odette was at first worried: were Sam and Caroline whom we had sent to our friends the McDougals in Michigan, missing us too much? "No," I suggested, "Don't worry!" "Should I call them?" "No!" I added, "It's too soon!"

The motel we checked into was composed of separate log cabins with complete kitchens in each and a free bottle of milk with the peel off tin tops like the old days! We celebrated our arrival with a bottle of New Zealand red wine—and jumped into the public hot springs nearby. "I feel guilty that I don't feel guilty," Odette said with a smile, refilling her glass. I smiled too. We needed this. All parents do. And we could think of no better place to be in than New Zealand.

Jet lag melted away as we enjoyed the springs and the night view of the New Zealand mountains surrounding us in the dark and the snow reaching up to a few yards from the Springs. Two weeks later as we left, we vowed we would return, with children, and do the real kind of New Zealand vacation: on foot, in canoe or kayak and in tents. Or, as they say, "tramping."

"Do you want any breakfast, Dad?" said Sam as the United Airlines flight attendant came by and the credits for the third film scrolled by in blurry video projection.

"Sure thing, where's the coffee?" I replied as daylight poured through the windows and Auckland and New Zealand awaited us in two hours.

SETTLING IN AT 11 MOIR STREET

Summer sunlight pouring through the small stain glass panels at the top or our bedroom windows. And somewhere outside, the sounds of Sam and Caroline's laughter as they explored the backyard in the bright sunshine.

My first impression of our new home in Wellington was one of space and light. Harriet's house was typical of New Zealand, particularly for the turn of the century when this would originally have been built: wood construction, one floor, windows everywhere and a corrugated tin roof. We were on a one-block dead end street full of houses of the same period but of different designs and sizes and each with a different paint and color scheme ranging from our simple off white to houses painted deep yellow with red trim or a rich dark red with white trim. Furthermore we were almost literally in the heart of Wellington and yet we were technically in Mt. Victoria, a suburb that used to be heavily ethnic and particularly Greek at that, on the slopes of one of the mountains ringing the city. Three blocks up slope and the houses ended and the forest began, honey- combed with paths and small parks.

After our life in basically two rooms on Kea, Odette said it best, "I feel so spoiled here!" as we unpacked. We wandered from the study to the bathroom and laundry room, the children's room, long hall way, living room and very large kitchen with adjoining dining room. That wasn't all. It included a tool and storage area under the house with an earthen floor that prompted Sam to think of archeological digs for ancient Maori remains. We could live here very well. And did.

WELCOME TO WELLINGTON

"There's more salmon and kumara for anyone who wants them," said my Kiwi colleague and friend, Russell Campbell as he helped himself to seconds in his attractive small home on the slope of another mountain in Wellington.

"Kumara?" asked Odette. "Yes, Maori for sweet potato!" was Russell's answer.

Russell is a tall, bespectacled fellow, with long wavy hair. In his mid-fifties, he is a documentary filmmaker, a fine film studies lecturer, an active member of the New Zealand film community on many levels, and a father of a brightly smiling three and a half-year-old daughter, Camille. That night was one of the evenings a week he got to have Camille, so Caroline and Sam were getting their first enjoyable dose of a very thick New Zealand accent as they listened to her speak of her toys and interests.

It was our first evening in Wellington, and we already had been made to feel very welcome. Russell had met us at the airport together with the film program's administrative assistant, Rachel, and had managed to get us to Moir Street with our luggage. I had met Russell when Odette and I had come through three years before and had stayed in touch since then. He would prove invaluable as a friend and as a loyal guide through all that I needed to know as a visiting professor at Victoria University.

Jet lag would kick in later, but as we sipped a tasty New Zealand red wine, we toasted our arrival and memories of Russell's visit to New Orleans over a year ago. "You will miss carnival season this year, won't you?" Russell noted. "True," I said, "but we can celebrate Mardi Gras here as well!"

Somehow Russell's home fit him perfectly. The bookshelves groaned with paperbacks of world literature and cinema books and videos. "Do you own your place?" asked Odette. "Yes," was the reply. "It was an old mine worker's cabin like many on this street and a group of us bought them and fixed them up before they could be torn down," he said with pride.

The evening light was fading and so were we as jet lag and a fine meal took their pleasant toll. How did we get home and to bed that night? A mystery still.

VIVA LA DIFFERENCE: DAILY KIWI DETAILS

Tena te ringa tango parahia.
(This is the hand that pulls the weeds.)

There are more people in Chicago than in all of New Zealand, this land of two large islands and a number of smaller ones, of an indigenous Maori population of roughly eleven percent of the whole, and with a government that was once a cradle to grave socially oriented organization. Now it has privatized not only railroads and electricity and phone companies, but has even begun to sell "highways!"

But for us, over the five months we were in New Zealand, it was the number of many small details of Kiwi life that intrigued, amused, and often impressed us. They include this random sampling of local traditions:

Garbage. Garbage was collected once a week in two flavors: all that could be recycled went into an official recycling green bin and the rest went into officially stamped black Wellington plastic bags that sold everywhere for a dollar a bag. Stop for a minute and simply begin to contemplate what effect this might have on the United States! First, you immediately start thinking about recycling because the recycling bin is free from the city, so you might as well wash out that tomato soup can and the wine bottle and the coke can and pop them in the bin. And if you are paying a dollar a bag to get rid of the rest, you really do begin to think about how much junk you generate in a week! Are you a two-bag, a three-bag or a four-bag family? Of course we couldn't help but snoop on the neighbors to get a feel for how "trashy" they were or were not. Yes, sadly, we seemed to generate a lot more than those around us but then our excuse always was that we have children, and except for a Maori family on the corner, no one else on Moir Street seemed to have youngsters.

Shoeless. Walking around bare-footed is perfectly acceptable. Kids, teens, and everyone else too. Sam and Caroline later reported kids at school barefooted, and it was a long time before I could simply get used to seeing, say a woman or bloke in their forties of fifties, walking into the big food store, New World, where we shopped, bare footed! And in banks, restaurants, churches. Everywhere! The custom has many implications, including the fact that the streets of Wellington are obviously glass free. But it also suggests a level of down to earth informality such we had not encountered elsewhere.

Post shops. The New Zealand mail also is privatized so that there are no post offices. Only "post shops," which are exactly that: shops that either carry other goods like a convenience store with a separate desk marked "Post" for doing mail related business, or a complete mail-centered shop that nevertheless sold stationary, postcards, and all manner of mailers, packing materials, calendars and more. There is, actually, much to commend this. For the Post Shop I most often frequented made it easy to "one stop shop" for milk, a newspaper, post cards and to mail that package to my mother or a manuscript to an editor.

Electrical sockets. And individual switches by each electrical socket. Does that save electricity? No, it simply means that no one gets electrocuted if anything accidentally gets shoved in. Obviously this safety factor is aimed at kids, but it's a thoughtful addition to the home we became used to.

CAROLINE AND THE SPICE GIRLS

In no time we felt comfortable with our new city and our new home. Wellington was a city in which downtown was only a five- to ten-minute walk away, depending on where you wanted to go. The waterfront was equally close, offering Oriental Bay beach and an indoor pool if you went in one direction. And, if you turned the other way, there was the Queen's Warf, which is a complex of theaters, cafes, a Maritime Museum, and various rental agencies, including four-wheeled bicycle carriages for four, like the ones we had rented in Santa Barbara in July. Also available at Queen's Warf were numerous festivals with live music, special foods and unusual attractions. That's not even mentioning the lively theater screen. For instance within two weeks in New Zealand, we had already taken Caroline and Sam to see a spirited production of Shakepeare's *The Merchant of Venice*, done in a 1930s gangster style and a Kiwi comedy, *The Farm*, about sheep farming and Russian tourists who want to buy a failing farm.

Activities everywhere. Several weeks after arrival, for instance, there was "Wellington Rescue Day" featuring rescue teams from all over Wellington representing land, sea and air rescue. But what was the special kick for Sam and Caroline? Helicopter rides around Wellington Harbor for $25 dollars. "Can we go?" was the cry. "If you pay with your own money" the answer. They flew without Odette or me and were thrilled.

Caroline found yet another reason to fall in love with New Zealand almost immediately. While Sam had a number of pop bands he followed and collected CDs for, Caroline had but one favorite group: The Spice Girls. While everyone agreed they were not big on talent—including Caroline—they nevertheless had captured her imagination with their sassy high energy working class British image, and so we all wound up during our first week in Wellington seeing their only film, *Spiceworld*, in a local cinema.

That in and of itself was enough for Caroline to feel that Wellington really was in touch with the rest of the world. But a week or so later, she was even more impressed to learn that three of the Spices had showed up in New Zealand on vacation and had decided to just start singing in a pub north of Auckland one night. The paper reported the old regulars enjoyed them but had no idea who they were, a fact the Spices actually appreciated as a break from being hunted down by fans throughout Europe. Caroline was amazed. New Zealand must be important if such luminaries touched down on its shores!

THE QUALITY OF THE LIGHT

"There is no twilight in our New Zealand days, but a curious half
hour when everything appears grotesque."

Katherine Mansfield, *The Woman at the Store*

What is particularly distinguishing about Greece that helps
explain why such a rich culture flourished there? The quality of
the light. That's the answer suggested by many poets and com-
mentators throughout history. The clarity of light in the Hellenic
world that has led to clarity of vision, thought, and of expression—
anger, love, laughter, and grief.

The light in New Zealand is very different. First, there is the
intensity of the sun's rays at this end of the world, especially in
the past ten years as a gigantic whole in the ozone layer has developed over this island nation, which New Zealanders frequently
told us with anger and concern. While we could easily stay out
under a Greek sun for hours, fifteen minutes of direct summer sunlight down under without heavy sunscreen cream was about it
before the skin began to color.

But there is something else about the light in the land of the
long white cloud. There is what I can only describe as a hard edge,
a metallic dimension that somehow more completely isolates
objects and people in a landscape. I noticed this not only on a day
to day basis around town and on trips through the country, but in
watching Kiwi films as well. So many scenes in films from *The
Piano* and *The Vigil* to *Sleeping Dogs* and *The Quiet Earth* feature
what I can only call a chilling light that alienates the figures in the
landscape. This steel edged light is not without its own beauty.

Yet it is a very different kind of beauty than the warming
Aegean light. It is, finally, the difference between the inviting simplicity of the smooth stone Cycladic figures and the elaborately
carved Maori wood demons and gods with their wide-eyed, wide-
mouthed, fearsome features.

STRESS–FREE LAMB, MATES!

"Glad you like it," our New Zealand friend, Joy, said, "but actually we would call it hogget, not lamb. It is a year old lamb, which means it is more flavorful than the so-called spring lambs that are younger."

It was late summer, that is, the end of January, and we were visiting a friend we had known for a number of years on a 2,300-acre farm three hours north of Wellington owned and operated by her "partner" (now the accepted New Zealand term for the one you live with and share your life with in all senses), Robin.

"But how do you get it to taste so TENDER? I mean it practically melts in my mouth." Sam and Caroline seconded that. And Robin smiled. "It's stress free mutton," he retorted, "because it was killed here on the farm." In his late fifties, his wavy silver hair and suntanned face definitely gave him the look of someone who had spent most of his life outdoors.

"Do you mean where a lamb is killed makes a difference?" Odette asked, agreeing to seconds. "Absolutely," said Joy, "Ever wonder why some meat is tough as nails? It's usually because the animal was transported somewhere, perhaps miles away, and all that stress of being in the truck, locked up in some pen, and pushed and shoved, creates a lot of stress and that comes out in the meat."

She had a point. And we all realized we were already into our Kiwi experience, learning what we had not known before, and sampling some of the freshest, and now we could say, most stress free food in the world!

The setting could not have been better.

Robin's house is an attractive and surprisingly roomy two-story turn of the century wooden home with a tin roof—so common in New Zealand—and a wide veranda wrapping around the front two sides of the house. The whole place is miles off the main road, Route 2, which runs to Wellington in the south and up to Napier and beyond on the East Coast by Hawke's Bay, if you go north. Behind us stretched the beautiful Ruahine mountain range, beside us a deep gorge with the beginnings of the Rangitkei River, which we had already seen miles downstream as a wide body of water full of boaters and kayakers.

Before dinner, we had gone with Joy out to some pastures near the house to feed a huge pig, and we attempted to track down Pete, the horse, in a huge field full of hundreds of sheep, dozens of deer, and two donkeys. Pete, a young horse that had distinguished himself by holding the New Zealand record for jumping in his age category—six foot, one inch—was playing shy and standoffish, however. So we left his feed in the field and headed behind the house for the aviary, which was filled with all manner of exotic New Zealand birds, such as the red capped parakeet, and others of various colors and shapes.

Utterly peaceful. And as we finally cleared the table and headed upstairs to our rooms, we all were smiling. One week in New Zealand and already we had an experience that put us at the heart of what this country does best in terms of its economy and way of life: farming in a big way and with style.

The next day would mean a tour of some of the property, beginning to fix in our minds a ranch, or "station" as they call it, with roughly 10,000 sheep, 3,000 deer raised for venison, hundreds of cattle, and, most important of all for Robin, many stud rams. With great interest we listened to Robin explain that as a South Islander from Christchurch who had never been a farmer, his decision to become a sheep farmer in the North was very much a chosen profession, and, clearly, one he had succeeded well in. For his farm is one of the top ram breeding farms in the country. He explained what that meant. That he worked carefully with the government to bring in new kinds of sheep, especially "texel," a new European breed. He quarantines them for several years and then breeds and cross breeds them, placing them with hundreds of clients throughout the country, especially on the South island, which he visits personally every year.

And how many full time staff on the farm? "Three," he said with obvious pride. My mind could not begin to fathom how such a ranching business could be carried out by so few. Furthermore, without a computer. Again, a winning smile. "I have no real use for computers," Robin replied, "I keep all in my head and I take notes on every sheep and every transaction. I like it better that way," he added, "Plus of course, my hours on the phone."

I counted over fifteen different bird calls as we fell asleep.

One week in our new country.

But this one would be different than Greece and the other countries we visited in Europe. For we would be here, down under, for five months whereas our entire European odyssey had been when all was said and done, four months. And we were already over the jet lag of travelling fourteen hours from Los Angeles, crossing an international date line and thus being nineteen hours ahead of New Orleans' central standard time. That had meant that we lost a day flying to Wellington but would arrive back in Los Angeles two hours before we took off, so to speak!

Sleep drifted over us. And stress-free lamb brought a wide smile to my face as I began to realize one reason I had so much trouble with fast food, hamburgers, for instance. Hey, most of those burger empires are surely based on the most stressed-out cows that ever lived on the planet, animals that were not full of "ihi," the Maori word for a plant or animal's natural excellence, when it is allowed to reach full maturity.

PLUNGING INTO THE PACIFIC OCEAN

"Who's jumping in the ocean?" I asked putting on my bathing suit.

We had checked into a motel two blocks from the ocean on the outskirts of Napier, a town that had been leveled by earthquakes in 1931 and rebuilt in an art deco style in the next few years, becoming what today is the world's only almost completely art deco town.

Sam and Caroline hastened to join me. But Odette decided to take it easy. "It looks a LOT colder than the Aegean," she said and curled up with a book.

In no time the three of us were on the black sandy beach that stretched for miles. Time suddenly stood still. Sam was already searching the beach for unusual shells and pieces of driftwood and Caroline was testing the water. But I was very aware how different a feel being on the edge of the ocean has as compared to sitting on the shores of the Aegean or Ionian Seas.

In Greece, you look out and take in islands or the mainland somewhere in the distance. Here the horizon was an unbroken line leading to infinity. Add to this the distance that New Zealand is to anywhere else, and the view from the Napier beach was humbling. There we were, Caroline, Sam, and I and an infinite cosmos stretching out before us.

I plunged in and though it was cold, the body did adjust after a chilly moment. With a lively twinkle in her eye and shrieks of freezing pleasure, Caroline joined me. "It's so COLD, Daddy!" she squealed. "Do you want to get out?" I asked. "NO, I like it now!" she said, and while Sam added more shells to his collection, Caroline and I reduced infinity to the pleasure of the moment we were sharing in the Pacific.

LONG LIVE FACULTY EXCHANGES!

Me haere i raro i te kahu korako.
(It is best to travel beneath the white hawk, i.e., a chief).

Long Live Faculty Exchanges. Not that New Orleans was under three feet of snow as we had arrived in Wellington in mid-January, but as Harriet began teaching at Loyola, Caroline and I had just returned from swimming along the East Coast beaches of Hawkes Bay, catching the last warm days before the start of the school season for Sam and Caroline.

The cheer of "Long Live" goes out to the very concept of exchanging jobs. For an exchange is very different from a simple invitation to teach or a grant to do research in a foreign country. An exchange suggests the joy of experiencing another university and culture, but doing so while also delighting in the on-going dialogue of comparing notes with your "exchange partner." That means while I began preparing for my film classes at Victoria University, I could e-mail Harriet and ask where to find certain videos or where she would recommend we spend our next weekend. And we, on the other hand, were enjoying Harriet's reactions to Loyola and New Orleans.

Best of all, was the education, in every sense, Sam and Caroline were continuing to get from our year abroad, this time experiencing another way of life in one of the world's most beautiful locations. That second weekend in New Zealand found us hiking, kayaking, and sleeping in borrowed sleeping bags in a well laid out cabin in a campground beside Lake Waikaremoana, high in the mountains of Te Urewera National Forest Park. There they also had their first contact with Maori culture. Over a hundred young Maoris gathered that Saturday night for what was both a music festival and a political protest in the park. These indigenous people were contesting a number of issues but especially land rights of territory, such as that national park, which they feel, with some justification, was taken illegally from them. And so Sam, and Caroline, began to understand just how complex racial and cultural issues can be even in such a relatively peaceful part of the world as New Zealand. This has led to evening readings before bed about Maori history, language, and culture since.

For me the exchange was also invigorating from the first week. Even though classes had not yet started, I was already impressed by the background many of the students were bringing to a class based on their applications for my Film History and Screenwriting classes. In my script class, for instance, I had several students who are working professionals who write for Shortland Street, one of the most popular New Zealand television shows ever. This situation would be a bit like having two of the Seinfeld writers in my Loyola script class! That would be a challenge.

Odette too was immediately charmed and challenged by what would be a five-month stay in this nation the size of Great Britain at the bottom of the world as she began to think for the first time in years of ballet classes and much more.

And what would happen when Harriet would back the spirit of

carnival to Wellington? Therein lay another tale to be savored after our exchange was completed!

KIA ORA: FIRST DAY OF SCHOOL

He kuku ki te kianga, he kaka ki te haere.
(A pigeon at home, a parrot aborad.)

On a windy warm late January morning, Odette walked Sam and Caroline three blocks to the Clyde Quay School for their first day of classes. They looked great. Sam in tan shorts and a GAP green short sleeve shirt and Caroline in a blue flowered dress and carrying a lunch box.

It had been seven months since they had been inside a school. Sam especially was a bit nervous. Not only were they gearing up for the whole school scene, but we were all still adjusting to thinking of this day as, well, the first day of the fall term. The previous week Odette had not only met with the principal but had managed the paperwork at the Immigration Office downtown to have Sam and Caroline's passports re-stamped with student visas now that they had been officially accepted into the school, an act that hinged on them seeing my official letter of "employment" at Victoria University.

And so Odette and I went about our errands during the day, eager for 3 p.m., when we walked over and waited for the first day to let out.

Sam was out first. All smiles, he was full of stories. "Man, they all wanted me to speak American and they want me to bring in some American money so they can see what it looks like!" he said, clearly enjoying his status as "special person."

"Haven't they met Americans before?" I asked, for Odette had gone in to get Caroline. "No! And Caroline are the first Americans ever in the school," Sam said, as surprised as I was too.

At that moment a boy Sam's age waved and called out to Sam and came running across the street to him as if he had known Sam all his life. "Your lunchroom change, Sam. See ya tomorrow!" And he was gone.

"Guess what, Dad," Sam continued. "The principal spoke to our class since we are the oldest group and said we all have to do some work for the school this year like helping younger students read or showing visitors around and other stuff, and our prize for doing this is we get to go on trips, including kayaking and SKIING, Dude. We will actually go skiing and they will pay for it!" I hadn't seen such a wide grin on Sam's face in a very long time.

Then Caroline and Odette were out, and Caroline was beaming too. "I made six new friends today," she said, "And we sang songs in Maori and my teacher, Fa'anu'u, is Samoan and plays the guitar." All the way home both were trading stories of what a great school Clyde Quay was. Odette and I smiled: our biggest worry about New Zealand appeared to have just melted away in the easy embrace of a good school. I cast an eye over the first newsletter they had brought, which began with the ever present Maori greeting, *Kia ora*. Besides the usual back to school notes, there was the following one, a timely reminder of the dangers of the hole in the ozone layer above New Zealand: "We would like all children to bring a hat to school during Term 1 to wear while they are playing outside. We are thinking of making this compulsory and would appreciate any comments."

"Dad, do you have any dollars I can take to school tomorrow to show my friend Sam?" asked Sam as we turned the corner onto Moir Street.

THE GREEKS OF WELLINGTON

"*Opa!*" shouted one of the four Greek women dancing the familiar village circle dance one sees everywhere in Greece. But these women were not on Kea or Crete or Ithaca. They were in Theo's Taverna in downtown Wellington, some three blocks from our house. We were sharing our first Greek meal in Wellington with Julianne, a friend from the South Island, and it felt somehow very comfortable to be eating mousaka in a country thousands of miles from the homeland.

What of the Greeks in Wellington?

"Kastos is the home island," explained Vicky Yiannoutsos, a New Zealand born Greek in her late thirties. We had been introduced to her several weeks before, and the video version of her touching documentary *Visible Passage* about her return to the family island in Greece continued.

"Now that's an island we haven't been to," I explained, saying that we did make it to Ithaca. With her own voice over on the film, she explained that this once thriving small island close to Ithaca in the Ionian Sea now has no more than fifty inhabitants. Her film documents several New Zealand Greek gatherings, including a farewell party for Vicky and another relative as they prepare to leave for the old country. In that seen we see a number of relatives speaking into a tape recorder for their beloved relative back home. Then when Vicky reaches the island, there is the scene of Vicky playing the video through her aged aunt's television set so that she can see her relatives in New Zealand speaking to her. The aged woman in the traditional black dress of mourning sits smiling, but with tears in her eyes, waving to the screen as if those so far away could see her.

Vicky, who is both a filmmaker and an acting teacher, lives and works out of Auckland, New Zealand's largest city, which represents almost half of the country's population. But in several visits to Wellington, she proved to be a valuable source of information about the Greeks of Wellington and, indeed, New Zealand in general. "There are only a few thousand," she commented, "and Wellington is definitely the center, though there is also a church and small community in Palmerston North where my family moved when I was young."

We lived on the street just behind the Greek cathedral, which was, appropriately enough, located on Hania Street. The street and the Greek presence in New Zealand were no surprise, for the two nations share much. Of course on one hand Greeks, like many from Southern and Eastern Europe, immigrated in large numbers throughout the early part of the century. But the largest influx of Greeks came after the First World War when several million Greeks were forced to leave Asia Minor, and then after World War II when many Greeks from Crete—thus the name of the street, Hania, after the city in Crete—because of the close Kiwi connection with that island. For the New Zealanders fought bravely on Crete against the Nazis, and many of them, trapped in the mountains of Crete for over three years after the famous Battle of Crete, hid in caves and were kept alive by brave mountain peasants and their families, who risked life and limb to bring them food and supplies. One ship alone after the war brought one hundred and fifty women of Crete, who came to work, settle, and marry in this land they had admired as youths, meeting and, in many cases, marrying, Kiwi soldiers.

Thus one dimension of our stay in New Zealand was getting to know better the Greek community of Wellington. This meant meeting the talented and energetic Tolis Papazoglou, who is Greek-Greek and one of Wellington's best production designers in theater, among whose recent works before we had arrived was an imaginative production of *Agamemnon*. He had much to say too, including more on how the community, once very close and centered physically in the Mt Victoria area near the church where we were living, has now followed the usual pattern of Greeks abroad everywhere and moved to the suburbs as they earn more money.

And there was Theo, the very pleasant Kiwi-Greek in his thirties who runs Theo's Taverna at the end of Hania Street, the pleasant restaurant which not only offered the best of Greek food and wine, but live Greek music three nights a week. On those nights Theo picks up the mandolin and another friend, who is a chemical engineer with a Ph.D. in chemistry by day but a fine accordion player "for the fun of it" in the evenings, joins in too.

The women dancing that night we first went to Theo's finished up and invited us to join them on the next set. But it was a school night, and we promised to return on a Saturday evening when they explained that "things really get going here!"

Theo and his friend were also eager to explain that the Greek community had big plans for the upcoming celebration of Greek Independence Day, March 25th, and that we should join in. We agreed. And we did!

SEALS, SEALS AND MORE SEALS!

"Unbelievable, Dad, real live seals!" Sam made the discovery first, and Caroline and I were right behind him. We saw the flippers of what at first glance appeared to be a small dolphin and perhaps a dead one at that, for the flippers were simply floating for a while until we saw the New Zealand fur seal right itself after foraging around in large, wide seaweed, and we saw his playful head cutting through the water towards the rocks.

"Look, Sam, a whole bunch of them," shouted Caroline with glee. "I can't believe it!" said Sam as we scurried quietly up to the ocean's edge and looked out over the large rocks covered with seals sunbathing, snorting, chatting, and, in one case, even skirmishing over a lovely seal lady.

Sam and Caroline had smiles from ear to ear and eyes sparkling as, for the next half-hour, they took in this amazing Kiwi sight. And I enjoyed them enjoying these creatures enjoying a summer Sunday afternoon, in their natural habitat, some eighty miles from Wellington along the sparsely inhabited East Coast near the fishing village of Ngawi.

Odette had been hit with a nasty flu, but Sam and Caroline and I were out for a Sunday in the country. We had driven up to Martinborough, a beautifully restored old wine and sheep town, which as we approached it, was hosting the All New Zealand Touring Corvette Group. What is that you ask? Just ask Sam. "Dad, look, it's what we saw in the newspaper yesterday, Corvettes everywhere on tour!" He and Caroline fell to counting and reached sixty-two by the time we were out of town. "Sixty-three," said Sam, finding one more to his amazement.

"Let's head on to the lighthouse," I suggested.

"Five more minutes, Dad," was Caroline's predictable response.

And ten minutes later we left the seals and the eight or ten other humans who had dropped by to watch. Then it was to the lighthouse not far away and, for the fun of it, up the 250 wooden steps to the actual lighthouse perched on a cliff looking out over the ocean. The wind in our face, the late afternoon sun on our heads and arms, and a view of the mountains we had crossed to get where we were. Over the mountains hung a series of long white clouds looking very much like one endless white cloud.

"Look, gang," I added, "The Land of the Long White Cloud. New Zealand, indeed!"

CONFESSIONS OF A SOUTH ISLAND SHEEP FARMER: "IT'S NOT THE MONEY"

"See those ewes over there?" said Earl, steering his Land Rover over a grassy knoll so we could look down into the glen below. "We will tag and mark them soon so we know which performance ram they have been matched up with," he continued as we sailed down the hill with Russell, my Victoria University colleague, in the front seat and Earl's wife Bev and myself in the back seat.

"That way we can keep accurate records on which rams and which ewes are the best producers," Bev added. Earl headed for the gate to the next pasture, and Russell was out, unhooking the gate so we could drive through. "People ask me if I use a computer," Earl continued as Russell rejoined us and we climbed another long slope, this time passing dozens of dairy cattle. "And I laugh and tell 'em I do have a computer and I sleep with her every night!"

Bev looks like she has heard this one often and thus matter-of-factly adds, "It's all in the careful record keeping for us. We're into performance, not volume on this farm."

Russell and I were on our fourth and last day of a four-day "research" swing through the incredibly beautiful South Island for a Kiwi film comedy we were hoping to write, tentatively called *Make A Joyful Noise*. Soon after I arrived in Wellington, Russell informed me that the New Zealand Film Commission had a deadline in two days for "Feel Good" comedy treatments—that is—up to six pages of a story idea for a comic screenplay. Announcements would be made in late March as to the winners. For the fun of it, the two of us opened a bottle of wine and cooked up a simple farce about a New Orleans black jazz band family who become stranded on a South Island sheep farm and have to play weddings and funerals and barbecues on top of learning to shear sheep in order to raise enough money to get back to New Orleans. So we entered the competition. And taking the chance that we might do the script anyway, with or without the Commission, we hopped on a Tuesday morning plane for Dunedin, the fourth largest city in New Zealand, and, with a trusty rental Toyota four-wheel drive jeep, headed farther south four the rest of the week.

"How many ewes per ram in mating season?" asked Russell who, like me, was a complete stranger to the sheep business. "That depends on the ram," said Earl who, with his wife Bev, runs a farm and stud business outside of Balcuthra, some sixty kilometers south of Dunedin. "A good ram might be able to handle a hundred ewes," he said, slowing down for another gate as I took my turn opening and closing it. "That is," he laughed. "If he is in good shape and doesn't get a cold or a sore back! Know what I mean?"

I had my video camera on him, catching every word for future reference. Earl, in his fifties with a sun-baked face and a twinkle in his eye, was clearly a man who enjoyed his work. That goes for Bev, too, who clearly is an equal in their farm work in every way plus being the mother of three grown children. We were now approaching a shearing shed as Earl continued, "You know if you sat down and added up the hours and the work we do with the eye of an accountant, you would definitely say, 'Get out of the sheep business, folks.' But that's not why we do it. It's not the money; that's for sure. It's a way of life. THE way of life I've known since I was a kid and learned from my father. Because what I know doesn't come from school or books, know what I mean?"

"Sort of like music or jazz, right?" I suggested. Earl smiled, "Yes! Those guys didn't study either, did they?" And Russell and I smiled too: jazz and sheep farming were beginning to come together for us.

What a trip it had been. Our first day out had meant driving to the bottom of the South Island past the city of Invercargill to Riverton, the oldest settlement on the South Island, to a much larger sheep farm run by John and Joan. Our tour of that 3,000-lamb outfit, now in its fifth generation of farmers of the same family, led to an invitation to the Riverton Lion's Club barbecue at an outside bowling club (as in British lawn bowling: NOT American indoor ten pins!).

That evening had meant a late drive through rain and mountains to the beautiful fiord-land lake town of Te Anau where we checked into our first of three motor camp cabins of the trip. We woke the next morning to a clear cool view of some of the most breathtaking scenery anywhere in the world as we drove the 120 kilometers to Milford Sound, a fiord of high cliffs and waterfalls falling into very deep inlet waters. Yes, we want our script to begin within such a setting! And so we avoided the large lake tour boat with the hundreds of Japanese tourists and took a small tour craft that was almost empty and allowed us the maneuverability to pass up to and even through some waterfalls that fell hundreds of feet into the sea.

The next day we centered our attention on Central Otago and the resort town of Queenstown on Lake Wakatipu. One has the impression of entering Sundance, Utah, or some other upscale ski, fishing, hiking, power-gliding, and jet skiing resort complex. But more interesting for us was the surrounding area, including the old gold mining town of Arrowtown with its well preserved old cabins of the Chinese miners, and further up a step valley, the much more relaxed town of Wanaka on the lake of the same name.

Bungy jumping? We did stop at the bridge over the canyon between Queenstown and Cromwell and take in this Kiwi gift to the world at the spot where it all began. NO, we were not tempted, but ninety-four others had already jumped that very day, each paying $99 (T-shirt included!) for the thrill of plunging 229 feet over swift rapids where a team member in a rescue raft waited to retrieve jumpers once they finished bobbing up and down. The oldest jumper? One employee said he remembered an eighty-four-year-old woman, and other fellow signed up an eighty-eight-year-old man. Would we include a bungy scene in our script? We'll think about it!

Earl had now reached their home again, set high on a hill overlooking the whole Southern Otago valley around them. Dunedin, the Edinburgh of the South, awaited us that evening, but I had one more question to both Bev and Earl as we thanked them for being so generous in showing us around. "What is the deepest pleasure in all of this and over all these years for you all?"

Bev emphasized Earl's earlier point: "It's not the money," and Earl added, "At the end of a day, it's knowing that you've done the best you could do. I don't know why, but I made up my mind from a very early age that I would never accept being just average. Just getting by would not be good enough!"

IT'S ONLY AN EARTHQUAKE

One late morning before seven in late February the whole house shook. Odette and I looked at each other, held hands tightly, and we could hear the house moving for a good seven seconds. Odette at first had no idea what it might be, but I am an alumnus of a similar shake while visiting Los Angeles once years ago, so I knew. It had to be a tremor, and we knew that Wellington is on a geological fault and long overdue for The Big One.

"Call 111," I said, giving the Kiwi emergency number.

Odette called and had a short and calming conversation and hung up. She was laughing, definitely a good sign. "The woman told me she is located in Palmerston North, that she felt it there too, but that I shouldn't call this number unless I had an emergency!" Palmerston North is three hours above Wellington, and I had heard Odette say, "Well, no, there is no damage, but I just wanted to know if it was an earthquake tremor."

We checked on the kids and they had not been shaken awake. Then we relaxed with the first cup of coffee of the morning. "Welcome to tremor country," we said and Odette laughed again. "It's only an earthquake. Don't call unless it's an emergency!"

THE MAORI DIMENSION

"POWHIRI is a custom associated with the welcoming and hosting of visitors onto the MARAE—the meeting place and symbol of Maori tribal identity and solidarity."

Cleve Barlow, *Key Concepts in Maori Culture*

Poet Allen Ginsberg once described America as "An Indian thing." Not to understand the Native American tradition would mean, Ginsberg suggested, to miss the essence of what the land and culture offers. In ways obvious and subtle, New Zealand is a "Maori thing" we came to appreciate on a daily basis during our stay. Take, for instance, the way Maoris have made all New Zealanders laugh and cry.

Every Tuesday evening we became habitual viewers of the Maori comedian, Pio, who does a half hour of comedy sketches each week, playing over a dozen different characters ranging from an old Maori chief and a Mrs. Doubtfire-like "nanny," to a World War II RAF pilot, a rugby player, a Maori tough street gal, and a Samoan singer, to mention but a few. How good is he? Good enough to run against Jerry Seinfeld, who was always scheduled for the same time on another channel. "We have a long tradition of Maori comedians," said one New Zealand friend, "Especially in contrast to the stereotypic dour, stern British sheep farmers who settled this country." And she is correct.

But the Maori dimension in New Zealand also embraces tragedy as this exchange from an important New Zealand film suggests:

"You're a slave, Jake. You were born a slave and you'll always be one." These are the tough words of a Maori wife, Beth, battered by her tattooed Maori husband, Jake, after their thirteen-year-old daughter, Grace, hangs herself upon being raped by one of her father's drinking buddies in the 1995 New Zealand film, Lee Tamahori's *Once Were Warriors*. Beth's pain and anger is not just lashing out at her husband, but she is also pointing to a fact: Maoris over the centuries often fought other tribes of Maoris and used the captives as slaves. Thus an important dimension about this extremely powerful family drama, which became New Zealand's largest selling film ever, is that she is from royal stock and her husband literally came from a Maori slave family line.

Adapted from a novel by Maori novelist Alan Duff, the film is a very disturbing look at the life of the Maori urban poor living "on the edge" in the Auckland area. Teen gangs, abused wives, incest, rape, alcoholism, and unemployment are all displayed in a melodrama well acted and memorable for its intensity.

And yet in a purely positive light, everywhere we turned in New Zealand, we saw the faces of beautiful Maori children, youth, and adults; found examples of their art, song, dance, and influence; and read many of their myths, stories; and even bought a book about Maori place names we kept in the Toyota so we could begin to understand the origin of town, river, and mountain names we could only haltingly pronounce.

Quite simply, the Maori dimension is absolutely a fact of New Zealand history, culture, and life. We met them everywhere we went, of course, and Sam and Caroline both had weekly Maori lessons in school. Wherever we drove we saw *maraes*, the sacred community areas and meeting halls with elaborately carved wood sculptures forming arches to the entrances.

But the Maori dimension in New Zealand runs much deeper. There is, first of all, the frequent newspaper and media coverage of conflicts between *iwi*, tribes, and the government over land, and fishing rights in particular. For the history of New Zealand since the whites arrived has been a complicated and often bloody one as colonists moved in and Maori tribes who had not gotten along with each other were suddenly faced with a new and more imposing threat to their very existence.

The Treaty of Waitangi in 1848 was the British effort to reach an agreement with many of the tribes who "signed" it. By that treaty a complex relationship was set up guaranteeing the Maoris their own land and many rights, including all the rights of British citizens with the understanding that the Crown and its representatives had the right to purchase lands from the Maoris and that

Maoris now accepted British law and protection under the British monarchy.

Despite the obvious room for friction, greed, and misunder-standing that the Treaty created, any comparison of, say, the co-existence of Maoris and whites in New Zealand to the brutal relationship between whites and native Americans in the United States, would immediately suggest how much more successful this small nation has been in working out a bicultural society.

I think we all as a family felt a particular interest in Maori cul-ture and its development since European settlement because we knew that our new home to be—Oklahoma—has the largest native American population in the United States, making up a good eleven percent, which is roughly equivalent to the Maori popula-tion in New Zealand.

Differences between these two scenarios, of course, are imme-diately apparent. Oklahoma has in its history been home to more than sixty Indian nations while New Zealand has only Maoris. And while America is so large that the government was able to more or less isolate tribes on reservations, usually on land that white set-tlers were not particularly keen about, Maoris depended so much on fishing that a lot of their settlements were near the coasts where whites also wished to settle. Thus they have lived in much closer proximity with each other, and, yes, with the expected level of co-mingling as well.

The result has been that Maori influences appear in a number of places and ways. Perhaps the most recognized "trademark" around the world is the *haka*, or war dance, done by the All Blacks, the New Zealand rugby teams, before going into a game. The *haka* includes the making of exaggerated faces with bulging eyes and tongue hanging as far out as possible. Maoris have always been for-midable warriors, and cannibalism was a respected and expected part of Maori warfare, given the lack of native animals before whites came bringing farm and domestic animals.

Maori artists, playwrights and prose fiction writers also have begun to make their marks over the years. Novelist Witi Ihimaera has not only penned his own fine novels, including *Nights in the*

Garden of Spain, Balibasha, King of the Gypsies, and *The Matriarch,* but has edited several anthologies of Maori writers. And Patricia Grace emerged for me as a splendid short story writer who can capture much of Maori life in only a few pages. With elegant simplicity, for instance, here is a passage from one of her stories capturing the arrival of spring in a modern Maori community:

> "The big boys make bonfires by the incinerator, heaping on them the winter's debris. Old leaves and sticks and strips of bark from under the pohutukawa and gum, dry brown heads of hydrangea, dead wood from plum, peach and apple. Pipiwharauroa has arrived."

AT 5:30 A.M.

I am a morning person. And I came to love 5:30 a.m. in Wellington. Not a sound in the house or the neighborhood. Water boiling for coffee as I listened to National Radio with its blend of 40s, 50s, and 60s tunes, farm reports, world news, gardening hints, Maori news, and canning recipes. It's a time to reflect and look forward to the day as that first jolt of coffee mixed with light cream hits you while the Carpenters or Joan Biaz or Johnny Cash or Glenn Miller tickle your ears. Soon I would be reading or writing, answering e-mail letters, or correcting papers. But 5:30 a.m. is time out of time, but it is also, with the radio soundtrack sounding like BBC, National Public Radio of the States, and your local country station anywhere, very much New Zealand of the past time. What will I remember years hence about my experiences down under? Certainly the quiet pleasures of 5:30 a.m. will rank right up there with the big ones!

CAROLINE THE POET

Caroline bloomed at school. She has always been the reader, often finishing a book a day, but Clyde Quay School gave her many activities to participate in and new friends to play with and bring home. Then at the end of the first month, we discovered another love of Caroline's: writing acrostic poems in which the first letter of each word spells a word down the page. An early sample was:

CORNFLOWER

Corn as calm as a sleeping cat
Often it is blown by the wind
Rabbits race in the rows of corn
Now they feast on the plants
Familiar flowers all
Line up in order
Over the flowers a deep blue sky
Watches the corn
Each seed waits for its turn to grow
Reaching for the sky

And then a few days later:

THE ROSE

The rose grows a stem on its bush
Here lies the pink beauty
Early in the year it's just a bud

Racing to grow.
Opening to show the beauty of a rose
Skies turn blue as the rose grows
Each day bigger and bitter till one day it sees the world.

TROUBLE IN PARADISE

"The chief result of recent events has been to bring home to New Zealanders a fact which they have not always seemed to regard as important: New Zealand is in the Pacific."

Keith Sinclair, *A History of New Zealand*

A day did not go by in New Zealand that we did not feel what a rare place this Pacific island nation is. Yes, it felt to us like a piece of paradise: friendly people, stunningly beautiful mountains, lakes, forests, wildlife and sheep, coastlines and plains, low crime, low population density, great food, lots of cultural and sports activities. And some of the best wine in the world. Add to this that we were thrilled with Sam and Caroline's school and I with Victoria University, and we really did ask ourselves, "How could it be any better?"

Look at the kind of daily rhythm we had established during our second month in Wellington. Sam and Caroline woke at 7:30 rather than 6:30 as they did in the States, since school began each day in Wellington at 9 a.m. rather than 8:15. And they only had four blocks to walk to be in class as opposed to the seven and a half miles from home to school in New Orleans. For my morning jog, I could, on one route, jog through the Mt. Victoria tunnel, come out the other side and jog down to the Bay, jump in the sea at Oriental Bay for a quick dip, then jog home through the downtown area, all in less than an hour. On a teaching day, I had the choice of walking or driving to the University to meet my film history or script classes, often having lunch with colleagues. After school, we often found ourselves down on the waterfront at the Queen's Warf where we could enjoy a stroll, or Sam and Caroline could try their mountain climbing skills on the "rock climbing" wall, complete with guide ropes, spotters, and special belts and shoes, or roller blade around the harbor. On the way home we might stop in the city library for some books or videos and CDs and a cup of coffee in the library café.

Other afternoons, Sam had guitar lessons or Caroline ballet and modern dance. Then supper and homework followed by a quiet evening at home or supper out with friends or at one of the many ethnic restaurants, ranging from Thai and Malaysian to Greek, Turkish, Welsh, or Chinese. Cultural events? Plenty. We found ourselves, for instance, suddenly taking in more live theater than we had seen in years simply because there is so much of it in Wellington, and most of it of immediate interest to us, including a Maori drama, Shakespeare's *Merchant of Venice*, a Kiwi sheep farm comedy involving the Russian Mafia, and a mother and daughter autobiographical multi-media performance. And this does not include our trips, hikes, camping journeys, and more.

Not all is as rosy as it first seems, however. Our stay in New Zealand made us aware of some of the emerging troubles in paradise. Take teen suicide, for instance. Cover stories in major publications, such as the *New Zealand Listener,* covered the string of Maori male teen suicides in one particular Auckland prison, while the University student paper focused on the rise of teen suicide in New Zealand to one of the highest in the world in the past ten years. That student article pondered if there were any connection between the de-nationalization of everything in New Zealand from the post office and the railroad to roads themselves and even the Wellington Airport, which was up for sale since we arrived. Whatever the direct cause, hundreds of white as well as Maori teens are opting for death over life in the new New Zealand each year, and that is a very unsettling reality.

The youth suicide rate is, of course, symptomatic of increased psychological pressures and economic tensions in a country that is going through profound changes. In large part the changes are those of moving from a highly socialized form of government to one of an almost entirely market driven economy with private ownership. There is, for instance, no more government protection for farmers and most workers, health care is not provided as freely as in the past, and university students must now pay for their education.

Add to this the continued influx of foreigners—mostly Asians—and a decreasing New Zealand home population, and you have a portrait of a small country that had at one point been mostly composed of white Europeans (pakehas, as the Maoris call them) and Maoris who make up about eleven percent of the population. Today the faces of New Zealand are very different, as a walk through Wellington reveals Korean Kiwis, Middle Eastern New Zealanders, and a new wave of immigrants from the former Yugoslavia, since the recent war in Bosnia.

Likewise, a day does not go by that some issue of Maori rights is not in the news. Protests over fishing rights or land management or government support for projects, such as building or maintaining maraes, Maori community social, and religious centers. To this list we must mention the Auckland power failure that occurred early in our stay. A city of two million basically without power for days. Why? Because the private company that runs the power supply for the area since the New Zealand government privatized the power industry had not been run effectively and certainly, in this era of de-regulation, with very lax (or nonexistent) inspection and review policies.

Did these problems make us want to pack our bags and leave immediately? Not in the least. In fact, I suppose we actually felt some sense of relief. New Zealand is not, after all, paradise. It is a vibrant small island nation with much to offer and, like anywhere else at the end of the 20th century, with real issues to face, discuss, and work towards solving. But as historian Keith Sinclair points out, at heart, most of these issues really come down to one of national identity: who and what is a New Zealander? And that debate is not likely to be resolved easily, for there is still the old school who feels New Zealand is "British" and others who see the New Zealander as a more modest Aussie, while others see New Zealand as much closer to North America in terms of settlement, assimilation, and identity: "New Zealanders are the Yankees of the South Pacific" writes historian Frank Parsons.

Meanwhile I had to give a call to the Film Program administrative assistant, Rachael about some film class business. She is a Jewish Irish Maori, in short, a New Zealander!

BACK HOME ON THE RANGE

"See where the pasture land meets the timber line over on the next ridge?" asked Charles, my New Zealand-New Orleans friend as he steered us up a steep hill on his four-wheeled ATV, which I thought of as a powerful lawnmower crossed with a motor bike.

"Yes," I managed, as the wind whipped against us and as I could look out across a breathtaking landscape of hills and deep valleys and see, across the bay, the South Island faintly in the background.

"That's where my new property ends," said Charles, standing in the "saddle" and leaning forward to give us the extra edge to make it to the top of the hill as we zipped past placid cows and nervous sheep. "And see that little observatory over there?" Sure enough! Here in the middle of steep sheep country sat a pint-size observatory. "It belongs to an astronomy club that comes up once a month, and I allow them access, of course, since it is on the property of the old farm I bought last year."

We were then at the top of the ridge pausing to take it all in. But I was looking at Charles too who was obviously a happy man. That wasn't so just a few brief weeks before when he went under the knife in a St. Louis hospital for a long postponed hip replacement. He had had a rough time of it. Losing a lot of blood, he had felt quite weak and disoriented. But that was all behind him now, and there at the top of one of his 450 acres of beautiful farmland, only twenty miles out of Wellington, he was definitely back home on his range, and the happy master of all he surveyed. He was, once more, baked a golden brown and had the lively twinkle in his eye I have appreciated over the years.

"Amazing," was all I could manage. Wellington feels to me very much like the most relaxed city I have ever lived in. But here on Charles' farm, on a high hilltop taking in the countryside, the sea, and the South Island, I felt I was suddenly miles and years away from the "stress" of the city.

Charles had only been back a week, and it was my first time seeing him since New Orleans. Our ATV tour continued as he outlined recent projects completed—a road here, a new fence there, new cows, more sheep, a fine barn—and projects yet to come. I smiled too as Charles drove on, negotiating bumps, boulders, ditches, and streams, talking almost nonstop.

Then we were back at the house, a spacious modern structure with commanding views of the area from the large windows everywhere. Gina was preparing lamb and also glowing with the pleasure of living in such an environment. "It's hard to get me into Wellington," Charles said, pouring an excellent dry white New Zealand wine. "There is so much to do here, including just reading and listening to tapes. I now have a wonderful series on American history that I completely missed in all my American years as a professional doctor practicing my trade!"

And the evening proceeded with the happy rhythm of so many evenings we have spent together: good conversation, splendid wine and food, and a movie to see and talk over—in this case a New Zealand classic, John O Shea's *Runaway*. But best of all for me was a sense of beginning to understand my friend so much more clearly now that I was living in New Zealand. Thus his stories of what it was like for his family to be on the last train out of Prague in the 1930s before the Nazis captured the rest of his family and the other Jews and sent them to their deaths. Accounts of his childhood in New Zealand, arriving at age two, with highly qualified parents who had to work hard like all immigrants, his father becoming a cabinet maker and his mother a math tutor and teacher. And then the good years of growing up owning a horse—yes, Wellington was so small then that you could live in town and have a horse—and simply going off on horseback for days at a time with not a worry in the world.

Charles has had his very successful career in the States, and now he feels the pleasure of being able to spend at roughly six weeks in a row what adds up to half of each year in New Zealand on the farm. Odette and I had first seen this lovely place on our New Zealand trip two years before when we had stayed a few days in the house, enjoying the serenity and beauty of it all.

It was late, and I had classes to teach the next morning. But I would return the next week with the whole family and Sam and Caroline would not only take to the place, but wander off by themselves, safely, even daring to take the little row boat for a spin around the newly created pond. "Do we have to go home?" was the cry when that evening and others came to a joyful conclusion.

NEW ZEALAND
AUTUMN

"If I am not a Russian," she demanded, "then what am I?" "Very probably," replied the tutor coolly, before proceeding with evaluation of the Russian character, "you are a New Zealander." Lila walked out of the class. "I am a woman without a country," she told them sadly the following Saturday. "I am a lonely voyager on a strange sea."

Maurice Shadbolt, from his story "River, Girl and Onion"

"On days that are merely overcast, I think of myself as Maori. But when it rains, I am Pakeha, soaked to the skin."

Bill Manhire, from his story "Some Questions I am Frequently Asked"

MONOPOLY DOWN UNDER: BOARDWALK BECOMES LAMBTON QUAY

"Trade you Lambton Quay for the Taurmaruni Railroad," I said to Caroline over a game of Monopoly in late March as the autumn winds blew outside."No way, Dad," was the reply, "Cause Lambton Quay is Boardwalk in the regular version," Caroline added, making it clear she was nobody's fool, especially when it comes to real estate.

What was going on? Very simple. Odette rightly sized up the situation after several months in New Zealand. "School, friends, videos, camping and sight seeing are not enough," she commented. "We need a board game for those dead moments when one really needs … a board game." And so we became the proud owners of a New Zealand version of Monopoly! Yes, all the rules are the same and all the streets in the same places, but only the NAMES have been changed to make sense to the down under crowd.

"If not Lambton Quay," I countered to Caroline, "How much for Victoria Avenue?" "Now that's a very different thing, Dad," she returned. And a deal was struck as fall rains lashed the windows.

AUTUMN IS IN THE AIR

On a crisp afternoon in the second half of March, I could hear Sam's skateboard before I could see him. And then he rounded the corner of Moir Street, perfectly poised, wearing his windbreaker against the slight chill of March and with his full sized guitar in its case strapped to his back.

It was a memorable image of "Sam in Wellington" but also of that subtle shift that had taken place in the weather: autumn had arrived. Odette wondered when we would feel "the end of summer" as Americans attempting to adjust to a world down under with a reversal of seasons as we have always known them. Yet that moment for me and that day for Odette proved an easy seasonal landmark: we needed our sweaters and windbreakers for evenings now and even for windy days.

That day stood out also because it was our chosen take off afternoon for a three-night sweep of the north central section of the island, complete with its volcanic mountains and thermal springs and lakes. More than that, we now had a tent and sleeping bags and were ready to make at least one of the three nights a campout.

Autumn seemed in the air for even more reasons too. I had been teaching for three weeks, had begun getting to know my students, and felt the term was truly in gear at the university. Of course, Sam and Caroline were fully into their school experience and shared afternoons and evenings with their friends. Sam had just had a three-night campout with his school class at a campsite an hour out of town, and Caroline had had a friend over to spend the night. Of course Sam and his skateboard had also signaled both a change in his behavior—he was almost a teen and was learning how to hang out with his "mates"—as well as the weather.

We definitely felt settled. Odette too had hit her stride as she took in some of the writers' sessions at the Wellington Arts Festival and began other projects she had wanted to get to once we were "at home." Autumn in Wellington meant we turned on the individual room electric heaters for a while each morning, that we turned back the clocks an hour, and that it was now getting dark by 6:30.

That Thursday afternoon we packed the car and drove out of town through rush hour traffic, heading up the beautiful western coast on Route 1 as a very choppy ocean broke in large waves across the shoreline. Sam and I had tested out the tent two weeks earlier, coming up the same coastline on a Friday night, and slept in total comfort in our dome shaped tent, which Sam erected in fifteen minutes by himself.

We weren't backpackers yet, but we were not the motel family we had been across America the past summer either.

IN LOVE WITH KIWI MOTOR CAMPS

"Get Sam and Caroline out of the thermal pools," commanded Odette from the Cosy Cottage International Motor Camp kitchen on the edge of the lake in beautiful Rotorua. "Supper is served!"

It was our first family tent camp out in New Zealand, and it was definitely going well. Sam had put up our "three-man" tent, which we hoped would hold four, in no time on our "thermal land" in a row of various shaped tents. Thermal land? Yes, Rotorua is the number one tourist spot in New Zealand and in large part for its Yellowstone Park type geysers, hot spa pools, and even its land, which is warm too. Thus with an autumn chill in the air, we would be guaranteed to sleep warm on toasty turf. I made sure Sam and Caroline were now out of the thermal pools where I had moments before been luxuriating, contemplating how hard it would be to get out and do ANYTHING afterwards.

Supper was a feast. Fresh green pasta, marinated beef steaks, salad, and a good Australian wine on sale for cheaper than New Zealand wines. Caroline sang the praises of Odette's cooking, while we could still hear a young German couple inside preparing a fresh vegetarian stir fry dish. Earlier they had been talking the way world travelers do when they meet up with a Canadian couple also travelling the world. The Canadians had been all over the South Island and, in fact, had been in New Zealand eleven weeks. They were about to head for Australia. The Germans had just come from Australia and had news to give them of how the surfing was in Sidney and what they shouldn't miss in Melbourne, plus what was happening in Thailand if they happened to head that way too. How important such meetings must be for those on the small budget, off to see the world!

Clearly the environment of the motor camp provides the perfect meeting place for people of all types and from all places. In the States we have campgrounds with tent, motor camper, and RV sites, and sometimes a few rustic cabins with community shower and bath rooms thrown in. But the Kiwi motor camps are special. I have been to a good dozen of them so far and each has its own personality. Yet some things remain the same: take the one we were in, finishing our meal at an outdoor table near the kitchen. The Kiwi camp of any size offers motel rooms and cabins which have, usually, bunk beds but no kitchen as well as "tourist cabins" which have a kitchen thrown in too. Of course they have the tent and RV sites as well. Add the kitchen, which, in this case, had three stove and cooking areas, plus a TV and reading room above the kitchen together with a swimming pool and three naturally heated thermal pools, each of a different temperature, ranging from about 110 degrees to about 138 degrees. Restrooms came with fine shower facilities and washing machines and dryers were on hand too. Cosy Cottage did not have a camp store as many do, but it did have fax and e-mail capabilities.

Our price for a tent site which enabled us to use everything else for free? Thirty NZ dollars, or roughly seventeen American dollars. As Odette and I cleaned up, Caroline was first over to the camp trampoline for a before sleep bounce as the stars shone on Rotorua. We slept soundly on naturally heated turf.

The next morning, the sulfur hot springs aroma awoke me early, and I wrote these words sitting in the car next to our tent as the sun rose over Rotorua. Odette awoke and made coffee, which took longer than anticipated. Why? Another conversation in the kitchen. This time, a Canadian woman with two sons—one Sam's age—who, with her husband, are sailing the world on their yacht for "two or five more years." They have been sailing for over a year already, doing school by correspondence courses, and, for the moment, anchored in Auckland "for the year."

Meanwhile I talked with an American fellow in his forties, who was traveling the Pacific with his seven-year-old daughter for "several years." What to say? Odette and I had felt we were taking on a lot just to be a family on a one-year, world-wide odyssey. But the Cosy Cottage International Motor Camp opened our eyes to a whole other world: those who are into travel as a way of life as both single parents and as complete families. We packed up and drove off as I left wanting to know a lot more. "How is the Canadian family financing their travels?" I asked. "I don't know," smiled Odette, "I felt shy to ask and I wanted you to have your coffee while you wrote."

DOWN A SLIPPERY SLOPE

"Do you think your brother is still alive?" I asked Caroline as she and I rode the ski lift back up the mountain at Rotorua after shooting down a slippery slope on the "Beginners and Intermediate" luge run. "I'm sure he's more than fine," said Caroline with not a worry crossing her crash helmeted face.

Luge? Isn't that the Olympic sport where participants belly down on small sleds that shoot down an ice-coated steep trench at speeds of over a hundred miles an hour? Correct. But this New Zealand luge for tourists is different. This is a plastic "container" you sit in complete with a kind of steering wheel that also has a braking mechanism. And the course? A concrete banked path that winds down the mountain.

This had been Caroline and my second run, and it's hard to remember when we had had more fun. Odette had shot down on the first run and declared, "I can't believe I did that. It is better than anything we did at Disney World!" Caroline pinpointed the reason. "I like it because I can control how fast I go."

The lift was pulling into view, and we could now see Sam, who had just gone down the advanced slope by himself. His face was a study in euphoria. "Dad. Caroline. This is the most awesome thing I have done in my life. Can I stay here and get a job working at the Rotorua Luge Run?"

And as we took the sleek gondola back down the mountain, Sam continued to share his new found ecstasy with tales of how steep, how fast, how thrilling it had all been.

New Zealand had offered him yet another surprise.

ACADEMIC LIFE, NEW ZEALAND STYLE

"Any further announcements?" I asked my screenwriting class on an autumn Wednesday morning. "Yes," replied Katherine, an actress and professional writer for the leading television series in New Zealand, *Shortland Street*. "The hit British stage comedy *Closer* opens Saturday downtown." Then I piped in and added, "And

Katherine is one of the stars. I hope we can all get down to see it!" That Sunday Odette and I did make it to the production and were very impressed with the show and with my "student's" performance.

Call it another Victoria University moment.

I taught two courses—Screenwriting and Film History—at Victoria University and thoroughly enjoyed my students and therefore the experience in both classes. Two courses would be a normal load for a full professor at most American universities. But as I discovered, I was actually doing the work of roughly four American courses, if you count contact hours, for the Film History class of seventy-two students met eight hours a week and Screenwriting for three class hours, plus I put in an average additional five hours a week for individual script conferencing, one on one. A lot of work.

And yet I had absolutely no complaints because I enjoyed it so much. Start with Screenwriting. Because the course really had not been taught before, not only at Victoria University but neither in Wellington, there was an incredible energy level around this group of twenty-two who made the cut from the more than sixty who wanted in. What to say, except that in all my twenty years of teaching screenwriting, I've never had such a large group nor such a talented one. There were absolute beginners who were eighteen years old and well-proven professionals, such as Katherine and Kate, a writer and actress in her forties who, among other projects, has headed up a hilarious and well known and loved travelling women's comedy troupe called Hen's Teeth.

A script class works best with no more than fifteen. That's partly because of the load on the professor to read the 120-page complete scripts the students are writing, and because of the group dynamics of allowing enough class time for workshop styled readings and discussion. But given the need for this class in Wellington, I willingly took on the extra work, the hundreds of additional pages, and the hours needed to conference with each every other week about their work in progress.

The scripts themselves? Quite simply this group represented a whole new generation of New Zealand writers, and it was exciting to hear and read their stories. No, nobody was trying to write a sequel to Jane Campion's *The Piano* or the Maori family drama, *Once Were Warriors*. I encouraged their own individual "voices," and the tales are ranging from those of a pregnant taxi driver who demands her clients tell stories as she drives instead of charging them, to one about two South Island, innocent sheep farm gals moving to Wellington and working in a massage parlor in the early 70s. Then there was a script based on a true life woman, again from the South Island, who was a kind of male impersonator Jessie James figure: she would dress as a man and pull scams, rob people, and live the rough life of turn of the century New Zealand. What will happen with these scripts when completed? Easy: I fully expect several of them to become feature films within the next few years.

That left my other class, Film History. It is your standard beginning film class with two screenings a week, lectures, and small group tutorials. The pleasure here is meeting a wide cross section of students with widely different backgrounds. We worked our way through East European and Soviet cinema, Italian and French film, the comedies of Buster Keaton and Preston Sturges, and next, Alfred Hitchcock's British and American versions of *The Man Who Knew Too Much*. If we take just this week with Hitchcock, for instance, it was both fun and enlightenment to bring in Charles Barr, who is a British film scholar spending his sabbatical in Wellington with his family as he completes a book on early Hitchcock. Who could ask for more than the lively lectures and discussions that Charles evoked for a young group, half of whom had never seen a Hitchcock film before.

And there was that extra dimension too that one can bring to such an academic job exchange: helping students who may wish to study in the States.

Knowing how much young Kiwis travel, I enjoyed this aspect of the job too. Now add in the pleasure of meeting new colleagues, plus the privilege of not having to go to meetings or listen to campus gossip and some sense of my term at Vic, as Victoria University is called, begins to emerge.

There is more. Take the twenty-minute walk to and from home to the campus up Vivian Street and then, at the top end of Vivian Street, up winding footpaths to playing fields to more footpaths and then to the film and drama building tucked into the side of the mountain that houses the university.

Final question: even with a pleasurable teaching experience, did such a heavy load allow time for my own work? The answer: absolutely. Besides the family time and travels, I managed to complete the second half of my new book under contract with the University of California Press, *Laughing Out Loud: Writing the Comedy Centered Screenplay*. And that's no joke!

SAM TURNS THIRTEEN: "STILL CALL ME KID!"

Sam and his seven "mates" charged into the house, piling their skateboards at the door and heading for the pizza in the kitchen. It was Sam's thirteenth birthday, and the house and backyard were alive with the laughter of young guys and the sound of pop music on the stereo. The party was in full swing.

We had just come up from the Queens Warf where we had rented two four-seater bike buggies that the guys peddled around the waterfront in wild abandon, especially since most of Sam's friends had never been on these bike carriages before. Caroline had a friend over, too, and they were joining in from a distance, enjoying both their own company and the fun of "spying" on the boys.

Flashback to the previous evening as Odette and I talked about Sam turning thirteen. This was a big one for us and for him, and we all knew it. "What does it mean to you?" I had asked him. And he smiled, "I'm getting closer to the time when I can get my driver's license," was the reply. The boy was becoming a young man, but he had very mixed feelings about the whole thing. Yes, it was fun to be one of the few really young folk at the Oasis rock concert I had taken him to a few weeks before. But he still wanted to take his pet toy lion to bed each night, tucking him in next to him in an almost sacred nighttime ritual. While the pizza feast continued in the backyard, Odette called me to the front door as she grabbed for the camera. What a shot: seven skateboards parked, one on top of the other, by the door.

The next day—Sunday—was actually his birthday, and I took him out to brunch at a restaurant on the pier overlooking the windy harbor. This was a father-son "you are no longer a kid" time, and it went well. No lectures, no speeches. But we talked about everything from how much he loves New Zealand and how he has gained much from our year on the road, and he even admitted he was in some ways looking forward to life in Oklahoma. For two things that were difficult for Sam were the thoughts of having to grow up and pain of leaving New Orleans where he had spent his "whole life." There had been tears about both, but on that bright windy morning in Wellington harbor, I sensed he had turned a corner. Perhaps with the help of his new friends, and with at least some understanding that his thirteenth year would be more pleasant than mine had been. He was fascinated to hear that even though my youth was full of good times, that particular year was the hardest of all because we had lived in a boring suburb of Albany, Georgia, where my father was stationed at a nearby Air Force base. I had gone to a tough school where fights broke out frequently, and where I can remember coming home with my shirt ripped from school bus brawls.

Sam was now our young man. That evening, however, before he turned in, he came into our room and announced, "I know I'm thirteen now, but please call me 'kid' for a while longer anyway, OK?"

"OK, kid, now get to bed!" And he did

THE LURE OF THE GREAT O.E.

"I want to come back to New Zealand when I'm older," announced Sam, "and do my O.E. camping and tramping all over!" As he spoke we were far along a tramping—that is, hiking—trail in the Abel Tasman National Park near the northwest corner of the South Island.

O.E.? Yes, every Kiwi knows what THAT is: an OVERSEAS EXPERIENCE. Because New Zealand is so far away from anywhere, it is a natural and, indeed, almost expected fact of life down under that the young wish to spend a year or two or three abroad before "settling down." Young New Zealanders by the hundreds take off each year for London, Singapore, Japan and the East, Europe, and the States. They go with little cash and much enthusiasm, working as waiters and waitresses, farm laborers, teachers of English or house painters. And they travel with flexible itineraries, open to changes of plans according to whom they meet, opportunities that suddenly open up.

It's the easiest way, of course, to get a conversation going in New Zealand, and one of the most rewarding to ask someone about his or her O.E. For almost everyone has a story of adventure, of richly divergent travels, of experiences from the open road. Clearly it is a healthy "institution" in every sense: the O.E. broadens horizons and deepens abilities to understand, experience, and accept varying cultures and individuals. The O.E. makes Kiwis citizens of the world.

"Great, Sam," we said, as we continued to hike with one breathtaking view after another of sea and coastline, forest and rocky shores, streams and gorges came into view. "And I want my friend, Nemo, to come too," said Sam. Caroline was right behind him, happy that the trail was finally leading downhill for a stretch. I smiled thinking of Sam and a friend, five or more years hence, backpacks in place, taking in this land of wonders at the bottom of the world. I felt particularly good, I think, that the spirit of travel and of meeting new people and customs had become a part of Sam and Caroline too. For they both had begun to articulate how hard it would be to leave New Zealand, a place they had made new friends in and had become completely comfortable with.

Odette and I had also begun to be aware of the "other" side of the O.E., however. I am speaking of the impact of the O.E. on parents at home who often lose touch with their children for months at a time, and then, of course, there are many young folk who do not come home or do so only many years later. One friend with a son living in England put it like this: "When a son or daughter lets you know they are going to live in England or elsewhere in Europe, that means not only will you miss them but you will not have the pleasure of following the growth of your grandchildren unless you save your pennies, hoping you can see them once every four years." That remark opened a whole other world to us. We began to better understand the complexity of life for our New Zealand friends who are blessed with so much in terms of nature and opportunities and yet who suffer from the distances real and perceived from "where it is all happening."

The Internet and e-mail have helped to shrink the world and give New Zealanders more immediate contact with everyone everywhere. "But somehow that's not the same," said one of my talented screenwriters. "We need to have a real screenwriter HERE doing what you are doing: talking about the possibilities of writing beyond these shores. Just reading a web site or chatting by e-mail with someone in Norway is not the same, for sure."

"And you, Caroline. Do you want to do an O.E.?" I asked as we took a break and looked out over the unusually calm April sea. "Yes, but I want to go to Sweden." Another dialogue begun as Caroline's independence and interest in the alluring unknown shone through once more.

TOP OF THE WORLD: ON CLIMBING GLACIERS

"I can't believe I'm doing THIS!" exclaimed Odette as I looked down behind me at our line of amateur climbers inching our way up one of the largest glaciers in the world. It was a brilliantly clear late April morning. And the four of us were on the Franz Josef Glacier deep in the Alps of New Zealand's South Island. "Wow," said Caroline, red cheeked, bundled up in a friend's ski parka, and turning around for a look and catching a view down the riverbed to the West Coast some thirty kilometers away. "So totally cool," was Sam's handle on his first glacier climb. And me? A feeling of total exhilaration.

Richard, our fearless young guide, cheerfully lifted his ice pick to point ahead at the rising peaks of bluish ice we had still to mount. "As you can see, we've cut fresh steps in the glacier this morning since, as usual, yesterday's steps melted already, so you should have no problem. Just follow me and remember to dig your boots into each step toe first, right?" With a perky bounce he was reshaping those steps that had, in the past hour under a cloudless sun, begun to lose their shape, as he glided up glacier.

I had a smile as wide as the glacier on my face as I held Caroline's hand and helped her up a particularly slippery step. We had not planned such an adventure. Given that we only had a week on the South Island for our second week of Easter school holidays, the idea had been to do a whole lot of driving so we could "see" as much as possible.

But our experience of tramping and staying in the Abel Tasman National Park had been so positive, we agreed we should slow down and do less but do it more thoroughly. Thus we would not even attempt two of the big tourist attractions I had seen back in February with my friend Russell: Milford Sound and the resort town of Queenstown.

"Take a break, folks," called out Richard as we reached the top of the Glacier's front. "Good chance for photos if you wish," he added. Odette who is the first to admit she is not an outdoors "type" and certainly not a hiker, looked relieved. No, she could not believe she was doing this, but there was clearly the beginning of a smile of satisfaction for she WAS doing it. "Yes, I'm a hiking wimp, but look at that water flowing through the glacier right there and realize any one part could collapse into another tunnel or hole at any moment."

And she was right. The glacier is honeycombed with little "rivers" flowing, cutting away at one level or another, and breaking into yet newer tunnels as this "living" hunk of ice does what glaciers always do: grow and contract, contract and grow.

The whole experience was a spur-of-the-moment decision the previous afternoon when we reached our cabin in the Franz Josef community. "Hey, the guided walks include boots and socks," I pointed out going over the brochure. That won Odette over, and we signed on. And after walking around the gift shops in town that seemed somehow like they were from Colorado or Switzerland but caught in a time warp as James Taylor sang on the speaker system, "I'm Going to Carolina In My Mind," we turned in wondering what we were in for.

We showed up at 8:45 a.m. at guide headquarters to be fitted for boots and given socks and raincoats, which, as it turned out, we did not need. By 9:15 we were aboard a brightly painted "Glacier Bus," headed up mountain with a group of about twenty-five. The second guide was Dave, also a spry twentysomething Kiwi in shorts, who was the Stand Up Comic of the two. "Right, folks, the hard part is the first part, the driving to the car park at the base of the Glacier. The rest is no problem. But to see if you are fit for the hike I will ask you to do a double flip as you exit the bus. Are there any questions?"

Immediately we began to understand how unique a glacier Franz Josef and its neighboring glacier over the next ridge, the Fox Glacier are. For we drove through rain forest vegetation, including thick ferns that reminded me strongly of sections of Kawaii, the Hawaiian island used for the shooting of much of *Jurassic Park*. But as soon as we got off the bus, there was a glacier a mile in front of us. That is the whole point. Most glaciers, such as those in Switzerland, are the product of long winters in high mountains. Franz Josef and Fox, on the other hand, are rare—there are two others in Chile that are similar—because they are produced by a coastal rainforest climate. Of course the other ingredient necessary is the presence of extremely steep mountains with a valley down the middle.

"Check out that waterfall, Dad," said Sam, taking in the heavily wooded peaks on both sides. "It's like a living creature," added Odette, as we began to catch on to the fact that this twelve kilometer long glacier that was a hundred meters deep at the point we had reached but three hundred meters deep further up, was, at this point, "in advance" rather than in retreat. "The glacier used to reach several kilometers closer to the ocean, but it has been in retreat for centuries," Richard informed us. "But from time to time if there is a lot more rain or snow than usual, it reverses itself and advances. And that's what phase we are in now to the tune of about a meter a day!" Sure enough, a record of photos in the Center in town over the past two years showed clearly how much the glacier had changed as it moves forward...daily.

"This is the most awesome thing I've ever done," Sam said, after climbing out of an ice tunnel Richard led the children into. Caroline meanwhile had struck up a lively conversation with a girl her age. And as we began to descend, I asked the girl's father what he did for a living. "A professional comedian for corporate functions," was the response. And I laughed out loud, on top of the world as a warm autumn sun beamed down.

That afternoon we drove through the forests and mountains down the West Coast quietly savoring our experience. Then Caroline smiled at some point as we began to turn inland and up-mountain again and capped it all: "Wouldn't it be fun to be able to climb the glacier once a week every week?" Hey, and this is a gal raised in below sea level New Orleans and the flat wetlands of Louisiana.

SAM TURNS A CORNER

Our swing through the South Island in April proved to be something of a turning point for Sam. In Wellington he was able to do what he could not do in New Orleans because of the high crime and general level of fear "on the street": he could become a city kid, sailing his skate board all over town and hanging out with his mates without a worry from us except to be back in time for supper.

But Odette and I had our concerns for Sam had made it clear that he was not happy about our upcoming move to Oklahoma in June. We had had many difficult and tearful moments in the ten months since going on the road and seeing the Allied Van pull away from our old New Orleans home. And that was not all. Sam was becoming a teen with all of the growth spurts and attitude changes that suggests. No problem. But we worried that, for instance, one of the basic pleasures of life, READING, was nowhere visible in his list of things he enjoyed doing.

Something changed during our week in the mountains and parks of the South Island, however. Sam suddenly came up to me during one hike and said, "Dad. Can I get my own pack in Oklahoma and can we get a two-man tent, too, so that when you and I go camping we don't have to carry the big family tent?" "Sure thing," I said. And Sam beamed. "I'm really looking forward to Norman, now, Dad, 'cause we can camp and hike and do cool things like that, right?"

How wonderful those words sounded. Not just because Sam was changing, but because they brought back moments from my youth, for growing up from his age through high school, I was in Amherst, Massachusetts, and camping gave me and my close friends a lot of pleasure.

"And canoeing too," added Sam. "No problem," I replied.

Then Sam grabbed his copy of Hinton's The Outsiders that Odette had recommended for him, and in the car and later in our cabin for the night on the breathtaking shores of Lake Wanaka, Sam was lost in the adventures of gangs of teens in the 1960s. In short, Sam had become almost overnight, a reader. Odette nudged me that evening, nodded to Sam who was lost in his book while Caroline worked on another detailed drawing, and winked at me. Yes, if ever a wink was appreciated, it was then. Sam had turned a corner.

HOW TO SPEAK KIWI

From day one in New Zealand, we all realized we had to adjust "English" as we Americans knew it, and begin to pick up Kiwi English. Of course, Caroline and Sam were the first to shift their pronunciation of certain words and to augment their vocabularies to be in sync with their new mates at school. But Odette and I also found ourselves beginning to speak, well, "Kiwi."

Here is my short list of ten expressions I found necessary to get through an average day:

GIDDAYE: "Good morning" or "Hello" as a run together "Good day."

GOOD ON YOU: "Great" or "Good for you!"

TA: "Thank you," and thus the same as the British use of the expression.

MATES: "Friends," those you hang out with.

PARTNER: "The person I live with but whom I am not married to."

Very important to know in an era of nonmarried couples and many lesbian coupled households we became aware of. When in doubt about "husband" or "wife," always go with "Partner!"

FREEZER: "Slaughter house." Not cool to make the mistake of telling a New Zealand friend he can find a cold beer in the freezer!

LONG BLACK: A double expresso coffee, sold usually at the same price as a single expresso! We came to understand that there are two historical periods in New Zealand: Post "café culture" (roughly 1978) and Pre café culture. Long blacks are Post!

ALL BLACK: The legendary world famous national Rugby team, so named not for the brown skinned Maori players on the team, but for the totally black jerseys they wear on the field. New Zealanders may differ in their opinions on many things, but on the All Blacks, all agree: They are beyond being sacred: they are what New Zealand is all about.

DODGEY: "Uncertain" or "shady" as in a "dodgey bloke."

UTE: A "utility" small truck. Something like our pickup truck, but with an open flatbed back with almost no sides to it. Very practical for hauling small loads on a farm or in town. And a word to know since there are so many of them.

Put it all together and speak a proper sentence?

Well, you might say, "Gooddaye, good on the All Blacks for winning again, and I'd fancy a long black, ta, for my dodgey partner and mates, before we drive out to the freezer in my ute."

NEW ZEALAND
WINTER

"He wanted melodies, not symphonies."
Maurice Shadbolt, *Season of the Jew*

"She liked the feeling of the cold shinning glass against her hot palms, and she liked to watch the funny white tops that came on her fingers when she pressed them hard against the pane."
Katherine Mansfield, "Prelude"

A COLD WIND IN MAY

"I'm so cold I can't feel my hands," said Sam that afternoon when winter blew into Wellington. Everyone told us we had been lucky with the weather. Autumn has had an unusually long run this year, and we had made it through April without ever putting on gloves or a scarf.

But the first Saturday in May became what we and all our New Zealand friends agreed was the beginning of real winter. A sunny afternoon that began as merely chilly when Sam left the house on his skateboard to catch up with his mates became a bitterly cold evening as a winter wind blew in off the Bay. Caroline had a friend over to play, and they wanted to get out of the house late that afternoon. The cold blast hit us as we opened the front door, and we all retreated inside to bundle up warmly against winter's arrival. We then drove down to the Queen's Wharf to walk and play at the children's area by the Bay as the afternoon light was turning silver and fading swiftly.

At that moment by chance we saw Sam and his mates. All clad only in their T-shirts and skateboarding down a ramp at the Wharf. "Hi, Dad! I'm FROZEN! Let's go home," was Sam's shivering plea. I smiled realizing that only a week ago he, Caroline, and I had been swimming in the ocean on the South Island with memories of similar swims in Greece in October. And so we began to walk back to the car. But as crossed the waterfront park, a richly haunting four-part harmony Pacific Island tune could be heard. Then we rounded a corner and could see four young Samoans huddled in a sheltered corner, practicing their beautiful island chant as the last of a metallic gray day faded away across the water.

Ole Man Winter had blown into town as our friends in New Orleans talked on e-mail of the heat of summer, the joys of Jazz Fest and the end of the school term.

LIVING LIFE AND CINEMA FULLY

"Coffee is on," says Gaylene Preston, a nearby neighbor of ours on Mt. Victoria, our Wellington neighborhood. "Cream or sugar?"

She also happens to be one of the leading New Zealand filmmakers, a busy mother, a dutiful daughter, a community and school activist, and, since we came to New Zealand, a friend. Quite simply, she has made some of the best and most powerful films from this island nation that I have seen, including the very moving feature documentary *War Stories* (1995) in which seven New Zealand women tell about their lives during World War II, both at home and on the Front. Odette and I had seen the film in Wellington during our first visit in 1995 when the film premiered and had never forgotten it, knowing that the project began as a tribute to her own mother, Tui.

I had stopped in on a sunny morning to chat and catch up on film projects of various sorts. But as I walked into Gaylene's lovely spacious old wooden home, so typical of Mt. Victoria, I was met with a beautiful piano version of one of Randy Newman's ballads. Who was playing? Her twelve-year-old daughter, who also happens to be in Sam's class at school. Ah! Once again that feeling in New Zealand that everyone knows everyone in one way or another.

And then Tui, Gaylene's mother walked in, smiling and gave me a good morning hug. I smiled every time I saw her, knowing I first "met" her on the screen in *War Stories* and that Caroline picked her out even before she was introduced several months ago because she too recognized her from the film.

Sunlight poured in on the books, video tapes, and art work placed, piled, and scattered around. It is a house that radiates a feeling of lives lived fully, richly, and joyfully.

I had not met Gaylene until we were paired on a screenwriting panel at the National Museum during the Wellington Arts Festival. But I was immediately taken with her as both artist and person who is so totally committed to her chosen art—cinema—and to life as well. Being a filmmaker in such a small country is not an easy task. And it's even rougher for women, as seen in the fact that Jane Campion of *The Piano* fame has moved on to Australia and usually calls herself Australian in interviews.

But through luck, pluck and a lot of energy and talent, Gaylene has managed to make a memorable string of features. These include a wry comedy, *Ruby and Rata*, about an old white woman, Ruby, and a hip Maori mother, Rata, and her young son, as well as a strongly etched docu-drama, *Bread and Roses*, based on the life of one of New Zealand's strongest women activists, who became a member of Parliament in her fight for women's rights. Originally from Greymouth, a small town on the West Coast of the South Island, Gaylene has a down-home infectious simplicity and energy that clearly helps her get over, under, and through the roadblocks and obstacles that beset any filmmaker and which certainly are numerous for Kiwi directors.

Yes, and she has a tough sense of humor too. "I had to go to two funerals last week for friends in the film business who committed suicide," she says handing me my coffee. And the conversation begins about how hard life can be in this down under "paradise" that others see in terms only of beautiful mountains, lakes, and forests for camping and hiking. Her daughter then began doing a spirited version of John Lennon's "Imagine" on the piano. How did she learn to play so well? "Her father, my former partner, is a jazz pianist now living in New York," Gaylene explains.

Meanwhile I thanked her for coming out to my film history class to show *Ruby and Rata* and proposed her own joyful theory of cinema, which she calls "Film Blanc," in opposition to the well known "dark" Hollywood genre, Film Noir. "Film Blanc means," she explained to my students who listened eagerly, proud to have one of their own speak to them, "finding a joyful sense of comedy inside a number of daily details which taken separately might not seem funny." The students had smiled, catching on to this refreshing theory of film and, yes, life, that goes against the much darker vision projected in *The Piano*, *Once Were Warriors*, and other New Zealand films.

"No new funding yet for my next film," Gaylene sighs, "But I will shoot a commercial in Auckland next week. So that will put bread on the table for a while longer." And then I continue with how she deserves to have some on-going university relationship for master workshop teaching, both for the good of the students but also as some kind of steady income.

The phone rang, and Tui handed the phone to Gaylene. She had other projects to attend to. Yet I left with yet another piano solo echoing through the warm sunlight, feeling that Gaylene truly lives a "Life Blanc," finding joy in obstacles as well as in opportunities. Who can do any better than that?

FRIENDSHIP BY E-MAIL

"Will you still send us Horton weekly updates when you are finally settled in Oklahoma? After all, most of us know nothing about Oklahoma either and we have enjoyed and learned from your Kiwi and Greek reports!"

Several such e-mail messages from friends around the world as our year on the road was drawing to a close made us feel good indeed. For as we traveled Europe and New Zealand, we had learned a lot about staying in touch with friends by e-mail. Think about it. Because we were traveling so much, we had to consider our options. I love getting and sending postcards. But when you add up the expense of buying them and paying for international postage, you suddenly realize you either have to limit your mailing list or cut back on food and other necessities in order to finance your mailings.

E-mail proved to be the answer. For not only could we each write letters to friends, but we also experimented with a weekly Horton "update" report sent out to some fifty friends and a similar report to family members. Many of these weekly missives were, in fact, earlier versions of this text. I resisted the idea of a group mailing at first remembering all those awful "yearly report" xeroxed letters distant relatives and friends include in Christmas cards. But once we actually began to try out the message to friends as a group for several weeks, we discovered there was a very happy rhythm that set in. That is, many friends responded with individual letters to our reports and we responded personally to them. E-mail thus became very "user friendly" in helping us stay in touch with friends everywhere. It became a kind of pleasant middle ground between a phone chat and a long letter by slow mail. And since the updates were actually earlier versions of this narrative, e-mails to friends also served as a kind of living "first draft" work in progress.

A year on the road. And as the century ended, it had become abundantly clear to us that the computer and its ability to reach out to the world had become a convenience that "worked" no matter where we traveled. We had been able to "plug in" on a Greek island and throughout Europe, but also in motor camps high in the New Zealand mountains and in airport lounges. E-mail had made travel less lonely and we were very grateful for this gift of technology to the traveler.

LAUGHING OUT LOUD

"How long did it take you to sell a script from the moment you started writing scripts in California?"

"Seven years."

The question was from an eager young New Zealand writer dressed in the baggy pants and oversized T-shirt that have become the universal costume for young fellows everywhere.

And the answer was provided by our friend Herschel Weingrod, whose credits include *Space Jam*, *Trading Places*, *Twins*, *Kindergarten Cop*, and other films as he fielded questions during a full day workshop on script comedy I had organized in early May with the support of Victoria University, the New Zealand Writers Guild, and the New Zealand Film Commission.

The location was a large lecture hall at Victoria University and the group of over seventy participants represented a feisty mixture of seasoned writers and a number of talented beginners.

Seven years? Faces dropped. Obviously many New Zealanders had hoped to hear how easy it might be to break into the big time, but Herschel's message was that of a seasoned vet who had paid his dues. What kept him going? Pluck and luck, a great sense of humor, and a love of cinema. Any more questions?

The seminar carried on for another hour, but I was thinking about the fun we had had for a week with Herschel. I had met him months ago when he did a workshop for me in New Orleans, and we had met up again in Los Angeles while I was teaching for Cal State at Long Beach. Yet having him come to New Zealand was even more special, for he had never been before and we all enjoyed being the "seasoned" Americans in this exciting and beautiful land.

Somehow Herschel's visit pulled a lot together for us. Yes, simply to catch up on American news reminded us we would eventually be heading home. But there was also a deep pleasure in sharing another American writer with students at the University and with our new friends. Herschel was only in "town" for a week, but he managed to have a grand time himself ("It's always good to get out of Los Angeles from time to time!"). And Herschel was generous is sharing his message: humor is important for us all, but it takes good hard work to nourish and produce!

Sam's favorite moment with Herschel? No question. It was Herschel's agreement to come to Sam's class at school and talk about Hollywood. Suddenly school in New Zealand became, for Sam and his fellow students, a discussion of how to join Bugs Bunny and Michael Jordan within the same story about basketball, one of Herschel's deep loves.

VOYAGE TO KAPITI ISLAND

"Look!" Odette said with excitement pointing to the clearing in the bush ahead of us, "It's a Takahe, the bird that is almost extinct. This is one of only two hundred left in the world and nine of them are here on Kapiti Island."

In front of us was a flightless bird about the size of a large chicken with a blue neck, green wings and an orange beak. It was simply ambling around with not a care in the world as we and a few more fellow travelers to this special nature preserve island stood and gazed and snapped photos. I am far from a devoted bird watcher, but suddenly I felt what a rare experience we were sharing in one of the world's most special areas, Kapiti Island.

"Daddy," Caroline piped in, "Mom and I saw some kakarikis while we were coming down the mountain." She continued, "They are green parakeets and in fact the Maori word for green is 'kakariki'." Meanwhile Sam was headed for the nearby beach, walking past several brown wekas, another flightless bird that shows no sign of fear of the few humans allowed on the island each day.

Only two weeks shy of our departure from New Zealand we were all thrilled to be on yet another adventure that involved hiking, watching, and sharing experiences. We had not seen any of the hundreds of kiwis on the island since they are nocturnal, but we had in our four-hour hike up to the summit of the island's mountain seen various other species of birds we could identify, including saddlebacks, with their red backs; the mimicking white throated tuis; tiny fantails; the large footed pukekos; black stilts; and others we did not know.

Yes, we had finally managed to visit Kapiti Island, a steeply ridged place some ten kilometers by two, which we had been hearing about ever since we had arrived in New Zealand, and which we had seen from the West Coast highway countless times. The trick had been both to find a free day and to go through all the procedures necessary to spend time on this island that is so completely controlled as a bird sanctuary that the Department of Conservation officials had over the past few years eradicated over 22,000 possums and thousands of rats to render the island entirely "mammal free." That had been New Zealand's natural state when the first Maoris arrived. Many birds, such as the now extinct Moas, had long since lost the power of flight for they had no natural enemies.

But the coming of the white man especially upset all of this as he brought not only sheep, cattle, deer, dogs, pigs, and cats, but two mammals that have brought on much destruction: the rabbit and especially the possum.

For us to visit Kapiti Island, Odette had needed to go down to the DOC (Department of Conservation) office in Wellington and sign us up and pay for our permits for a six-hour day's visit ($6 each). DOC only allows fifty visitors a day to keep the island from becoming overrun by people, even if they are "eco-tourists." Then we had booked a boat ride by phone and had double checked at 7 a.m. that Saturday morning to make sure the ocean was calm enough for the boat to take off at 9 a.m. for the fifteen-minute ride across.

"Check out the tractor and the boat," Sam had said when we drove up to the departure point on the coast. With early winter morning sunshine and no wind, in a parking lot by the beach, we climbed on board a small motor boat that could hold about twenty if full, and a huge tractor dragged us into the water so we could head on out since there is no wharf at that part of the beach.

Our captain was John, a Maori in his mid-thirties, who was also our official guide to the island. A sturdy fellow with the typical Kiwi shorts and short hair, he had a wealth of knowledge about the flora and fauna of Kapiti, not only because he had studied it, but because he had lived on the island for several years when he was younger.

"Maoris have lived on the island for at least several hundred years," he told me as we sped towards the beach at the center of the island's coastline. "And when this became a special preserve at the turn of the century, it was arranged that the Maori families living here on what is about 20 percent of the land, could continue to do so forever if passed on to blood members of the families."

In fact, the only other passengers on the boat were a Maori woman from the South Island and her cute sixteen-month-old son whom she was taking to see his grandfather on the island for the first time. "It will be an emotional day," she smiled, "For my father has never seen his grandson." Suddenly our journey was much more than just that of heading into a wilderness to watch rare birds. We were sharing a Maori family odyssey.

But there was another passenger. Tonaia Baker is a Maori woman in her sixties, who, as just a few minutes of conversation revealed, is a filmmaker specializing in documentaries about

Maoris but also about the New Zealand whales, which almost became extinct as well. "My family goes back six generations on Kapiti and I am coming out for the day to visit before I go on another shoot in Auckland tomorrow."

I had to smile. Here in the middle of New Zealand's most unspoiled location, I run into a fellow filmmaker, but not just that, a filmmaker who is from the place we are visiting and who, as it turned out, knew a filmmaking friend of ours in Louisiana who had made a documentary on whales.

We landed on the rocky beach as John and a crewmember held the metal gangplank for us and as a second boat carrying some twenty other visitors also appeared. John then led us inland a little and gave us all an orientation talk in a DOC shelter that also appeared to be a marae with Maori carvings on the front of it in the tradition of maraes. The rules were simple: don't take anything off the island except whatever we have brought onto the island and stay on the paths that lead along the coast and up the mountain and down. He also gave us a history of the island, pointing out that, "While the island looks today like New Zealand would have looked to the first humans to arrive, Kapiti was not always like this. In fact when it became a preserve in 1897, about ninety percent had been cleared and farmed as well as being used as a whaling station for killing whales and melting down their oil."

We all hiked through the bush and forest, hearing numerous different bird calls and fully appreciating how unusual it was not to see a single animal. Then Sam and I made the final climb to the summit while Odette and Caroline headed back down. From the top we could look out to the horizon past the sharp cliffs below us. And far beyond what we could see lay the next land hundreds of miles away, Antarctica itself!

"Oh, my god!" exclaimed Odette on the return voyage to the mainland.

The wind had come up and the waves splashed into the boat as we decided to don the life preservers that our Maori fellow passengers ignored. "How was the meeting of grandfather and grandson?" I asked the Maori mother as waves crashed about and the magical Kapiti faded behind us.

She smiled. "Grandpa wants his grandson to come back and stay so he can take him fishing and teach him a thing or two." And I smiled too. The traditions would continue from one generation to the next on this island protected from mammals and developers where this young boy would learn what it is to fall asleep at night to the exotic cries of kiwis.

ODETTE'S WELLINGTON

"Pick up three pounds of fresh salmon and some more red wine and garlic," Odette said as she handed me a shopping list for New World, the large food chain grocery store we shopped at down near the harbor. We had some friends coming for dinner as we did at least twice a week, and it was my turn to shop.

As I headed the Toyota towards the store through our Mt. Victoria neighborhood, I was thinking of Odette. How had her experience been in New Zealand? On one hand she had shared everything we had done together as a family. On the other hand, she had her own perspective given a health problem that had developed and the fact that she had not had to head for the classroom each morning as she had done the past four years.

We had many talks over the months about how she felt. She put it well. There was the keen enjoyment of "time off" that this year on the road had given us. A pleasure and a gift to be treasured while it unfolded and in the years to come. And the "time off" had meant freedom from not only a regular job for her, but also from "regular" social pressures. Because we were passing through, we only had to entertain those we wished to invite and spend time with. Thus the salmon were for good new friends and not a chore to think about preparing.

Odette had also enjoyed spending more time with Sam and Caroline and seeing that they got to and from their friends' houses and activities. This led to a decision about our first months ahead of us in Oklahoma. Instead of rushing to get a job, she felt and I agreed, that it was far more important to take it easy and help our children settle in and adjust to a new home, a new town, a new school system, and locale. This decision, made early on in our New Zealand experience helped Odette feel even better about enjoying Wellington.

But Odette had her moments of doubting too. "I haven't made as much of this experience as I should have," she said several weeks before we left. "I should have read more, gone for walks with you as you had suggested, DONE MORE." I laughed. "Hey, slow down. It's easy to whip yourself about things not done. But you have enjoyed it here, right?"

"Right," said Odette.

"Then nothing else matters," I added.

A cold wind was blowing as Odette headed to Clyde Quay to pick up Caroline. "A fire in the fireplace tonight?" she asked.

"No problem," I replied, and that evening over fresh New Zealand salmon (who said that lamb was all this country produced!) a Greek salad and a hearty red wine, we warmed ourselves by a fire with new friends.

"There is another way New Zealand has been important for me," Odette said that night, long after Sam and Caroline had gone to sleep and the last dish had been placed in the dishwasher. "And that is as a chance to do some real planning for our life in Oklahoma. What do you think of these kitchen shelf plans?" Odette handed me wonderfully detailed drawings of our kitchen she had made after e-mailing our real estate agent in Oklahoma for measurements and then her sister in law in New Orleans for her professional remodeling advice.

"Lookin' good!" I said, sleepily, "But will our table really fit in that space?"

"Yes! I had Marlise measure the kitchen and…"

But I was already drifting off back to dreams of climbing glaciers.

CHATTING WITH LOUIS ARMSTRONG

"What did I do to be so BLACK AND BLUE?"

The singing and the voice were familiar.

I was walking back home one wintry day after a film class in which we had viewed Spike Lee's *Do The Right Thing*. And I heard that mellow soothing deep voice ringing out clearly somewhere not too far away. Rounding a corner on Vivian Street, I saw him standing there, trumpet in hand, as if doing a street concert for the evening commuters going home.

"Louis Armstrong, I presume," I managed.

"You got that right, my friend," he replied, wrapping his worn scarf around his neck.

"What are YOU doing here?" I asked. He laughed with that distinctive chuckle. "Hey, my fellow New Orleanian, I manage to get around, you know. Didn't I make it to Yugoslavia once?"

"That's true."

"And Africa and of course all over Europe and Russia."

"I know, I know, Louis. You were one of the best ambassadors we ever had, spreading good will everywhere. But I didn't know you made it to New Zealand."

"Don't look so surprised, man! Musicians, entertainers, writers, hey, we all travel," he said, laughing. "And that was before there was any such thing as frequent flyer miles and stuff like that. I mean, did you know Will Rogers really got his start in an Auckland circus act or that Mark Twain checked out this country that was even younger than we were."

"You're kidding. Will and Mark made it here too? But when were you...originally here?"

"Oh, it was back in the 1950s and we played in Upper Hutt, if I remember correctly, among other places, of course. Wow, it was a pretty roll-up-the-street-at-9 p.m. kinda place back then, I can tell ya, but they loved the music all right. I remember doin' an especially long and slow version of 'Do You Know What It Means To be Miss New Orleans' when it was ladies' choice, and a lot of shy Kiwis didn't seem so shy by the end of the dance!"

More laughter. A woman in a Holden who would have been a teen when Louis visited last waved as she drove by.

"Louis, I've been on the road a year with my family. We started in New Orleans and in a week, we will return to New Orleans. May I ask you, in all your travels, what did you enjoy most?"

He blew on his hands in an effort to keep them warm and did a kind of a rumba to warm his body. "That's easy, my friend. Meetin' the people. Just meetin' and talkin' and eatin' and drinkin' too with...people. What else is there, right?"

I smiled. "What about the sights and...sites?"

"Oh, hell, man. I'm not much of a tourist. Never was. I'm a people man! That's what my music is all about. It's a way of sharin' and carin'. Get my point?"

"Yeah, Louis. Got it!"

"I kinda like what ole Duke Ellington said at my funeral when I...well, when I passed to that Great Band in the Sky."

Suddenly Duke's lines came back to me from a large exhibit dedicated to Louis that had been held at the New Orleans Museum of Art a few years before and I said them along with Louis, "Louis was born poor and died rich and never hurt anybody on his way through."

I had a tear in my eye as I waved goodbye.

"See you around, friend," he said and I agreed. Louis began to lift his trumpet to his lips again, but first he turned to me and said, "Say hello to New Orleans when you all go back. I sure do miss the place. Red beans and rice, yeah!" And he swung into a spicy version of "Down By the Riverside."

THE JOYS OF NEW ZEALAND PROSE

"This place need not be a place of old bones and grief."
Maurice Shadbolt in *Season of the Jew*

New Zealand woke in me once more the sheer pleasure of reading good prose. I had already discovered the pleasures of some of the contemporary authors, such as the Maori writer Witi Ihimaera, on our first voyage to New Zealand three years before. But this trip was to be a joy in part because of reading a lot of short fiction and complete novels by authors from this small but fertile literary world.

A convenient starting point was the anthology *Six By Six*, edited by Bill Manhire, the professor of creative writing at Victoria University who became a good friend during our stay. This volume contained memorable stories by Katherine Mansfield who is, no doubt, New Zealand's best known author outside of the country. But I was also introduced to the works of Frank Sargeson, Maurice Duggan, Janet Frame, the Maori writer Patricia Grace, and Owen Marshall.

I then found myself seeking out further pieces by each, including Maurice Shadbolt's *Season of the Jew*. To mention but just this one historical novel is to hint at the riches of Kiwi prose writers. Here is a stunning work that builds on a historical incident on the North Island, when an "outlaw" Maori leader named Kooti led hundreds of followers in what became a new fusion of Maori and Old Testament traditions in the second half of the 19th century. Kooti was never captured, but hundreds died in battles and skirmishes before he finally died and his legend lives on. The book is told through the perspective of a white farming ex-soldier, Fairweather, who admires Kooti but wishes to help the settlers as well. Caught in the middle in a no-win series of conflicts, Fairweather rides out the rough political and cultural weather around him as the tale builds in Shadbolt's steady hands to a tragic conclusion.

I was impressed not just with the telling of such an epic tale, but also with the way Shadbolt can turn a phrase, catch a moment, sum up an attitude. Fairweather says at one point, advising against a slaughter, "Let your last act of war be seen as kindness," and he describes himself at one point as, "A drunkard, yes. A fornicator, often. A coward, on occasion, a good less man, always, but a hireling, NEVER." And war is given a brief description by the conflicted main protagonist: "It is something that enables men to feel important."

Of course the screenwriter in me saw countless possibilities for new New Zealand films! But on the immediate front, I find myself often recommending these works to my American friends. I have, in short, become an ambassador for New Zealand fiction.

CAROLINE'S FAMILY NEWSLETTERS

It was Caroline's idea all the way: a family newsletter worked out on the computer each week, titled the HORTON HERALD and summing up what we had done that week. Odette helped her some with the computer graphics, but Caroline was right there writing away. And who was the audience? Just the four of us! Well, and then with her permission, we were able to send it on to my mother, Odette's stepmother "Gigi," and a few others. No, publication did not make it past a few weeks, but that's not the point. What counted once more was Caroline's vision and energy.

Here is one entry from the first issue.

"As everyone knows, we just got back from our trip in the South Island. We first went to Nelson where we met Julianne at the State Cinema. She kindly escorted us to her house. We then met her husband Bing and son Matthew. We then went in to her house and had a drink, some mussels, and nuts. Then we had a nice dinner of pumpkin soup, a kind of fish with a lemon sauce, salad and ice cream. We talked a little then got in to our bed clothes and went to bed. We woke early had breakfast then we drove to Kaiteriteri, where we caught the fairyboat to Bark Bay where we stayed for a while. Then we hiked for three or four hours to Awora Lodge. Once we reached the lodge we got our room and had some hot chocolate milk and coffee. We relaxed because we were hobbled, we read, and got into bed. We took a shower then went to dinner. Sam and I had chili bean burrito and Mom and Dad had fettuccini. We then went to the room to get ready for bed. Mommy read us some of *The Outsiders*, the book Sam is reading. We slept for twelve hours!"

WHEN OLD FRIENDS GATHER

"Would you like a little Greek salad?" I heard a familiar voice in Greek say as I turned in surprise. There before me was Vasso adding the olive oil to one of her incomparable Greek salads as Argiris, smiling to Caroline and Sam, pulled a roasted lamb off the spit.

But that was not the only surprise, for this comfortable little hall that doubled as the home base for a local Scottish bagpipe band was full of about thirty of our good friends we had seen during the past year. Odette couldn't believe it either as Carolyn and Henry from the Cotswolds came up and as Rachid and Katherine from France came in carrying French bread as George Szomjas of Hungary and Srdjan Karanovic from Serbia sat in a corner speaking of new films they wished to make.

How was this possible? For Penny and Costa from Athens; Louis Todorovic from the Broadcast Academy in Switzerland; Kevin Rabalais, Raiza and Claudio and the MacDonalds from New Orleans; together with Guianna from Padua; Slobodanka from Belgrade; Chantal and Jim Haynes from Paris; Homer, the movie projectionist from Ithaca; Stephanos and Katerina from Kea; and Antonis Samarakis and Lakis from Greece were all chatting away happily as we entered.

Suddenly a New Orleans jazz band began to play as all our New Zealand friends also joined in, coming into the hall from several side doors. Our week in New Zealand had been both a pleasurable conclusion to our enjoyable Wellington stay and, at the same time, a tearful realization that our year on the road was drawing to a close. How was it possible that only a few days before leaving, all our friends we had met up with during the year had suddenly shown up in New Zealand to bid us farewell?

Tolis, our theatrical designer friend from Wellington refilled my glass and winked. "Ah, anything is possible, Andy, you know that."

"Yes, but who organized all of this?" I asked.

Costa Botes, a Greek-New Zealand filmmaker, now joined me, "Well, remember the end of Nikos Kazantzakis' *Odyssey: A Modern Sequel* when Odysseus sails in a kayak to Antarctica and just before he dies, all of his friends he has ever met in his life and on his travels, come to greet him and say goodbye."

"Hey," I objected, "Are you suggesting I'm ready to die?"

"Not at all," said Rachel from the Film Studies Office, as Andrew, my teaching assistant began to serve the red beans and rice. "But this is our farewell party for you and Odette and the children," she added.

"Thank you all," I said loudly, "And I would like to make a toast to…"

Just then Odette woke me up. "Who are you toasting in your sleep?" she said, as the morning light came through our Moir Street window.

"Ah, never mind," I replied. "It was just a dream. And a very festive one at that."

MAKE A JOYFUL NOISE

We were at Russell's house again, just as we had been when we had arrived in January. And Camille, his Shirley Temple-like three-year-old daughter, was there too, again just as on that summer day in January, delighting us all. It was cold outside now in June, but the aroma of a special pasta dish filled his comfortable home as we met, for the first time, Camille's mother, Jane. More than any other event during our last week in New Zealand, that evening at Russell's gave us a warm feeling of the circle closing and our down under adventure drawing to a close.

As the conversation and wine flowed, I thought of the fun I had had with Russell researching and writing our screenplay, *Make A Joyful Noise*, about a New Orleans jazz band stuck on a South Island sheep farm. We had had our South Island "research tour" in February and had finished the whole script by mid May. It had been handed in to Neville, our producer, who now had the job of shepherding it into production. Plans were made for his visit to the States to see New Orleans, to meet musicians who could carry out the acting roles of the script, and to see about the possibilities of an American director coming on board.

Russell opened another bottle of wine as winter winds blew outside.

New Zealand had proved a most fruitful "work" time for me on my writing projects as well. I had completed the second half of my new book, which I had begun in Greece, on writing screen comedy. And I had even gotten back from my publisher, the University of California Press some glowing "readers" reports on the manuscript.

New Zealand had definitely proved conducive to that balance between work and pleasure, family life and professional obligations that we dream of but seldom achieve in practice.

"Now for dessert!" announced Russell as Odette and Jane helped clear the table.

ON LEAVING NEW ZEALAND: BETWEEN "TAPU" AND "NOA"

We were leaving Wellington in a few brief hours.

"I'm not leaving," said Caroline, who claims she would stay another six months and then return. "My friends' parents say I can come back any time and stay with them," said Sam, and we have heard the same from them ourselves.

The past few days had been an emotional roller coaster as

school parties for the kids took place, as "final" gatherings had occurred and as Sam and Caroline had gone through the process of packing up once more.

Yes, in half an hour I would wake Odette, Sam, and Caroline and a twenty-seven-hour odyssey back to New Orleans would begin. That is, we would fly to Auckland, meeting Serbian friends who left the Balkans in disgust during the War, and then on to Los Angeles to have lunch with our friends Sam and Harriet during a five-hour layover, arriving in California hours before we had taken off from New Zealand (ah! the fun of reversing the international date line!).

Five beautiful months had sped by in the Land of the Long White Cloud. And we each were carrying back special memories of friends, of nature, of schools and universities, meals shared, adventures undertaken, and discoveries made.

Farewells had been made and taken. But our last night we had a quiet evening together as a family by a roaring fire in the fireplace as a howling winter Wellington wind lashed the house outside. Odette and I shared the best bottle of white wine we had had in the past year of travels in Europe, America, and New Zealand, as Sam and Caroline delighted in singing songs they had learned at school in Maori.

Just another Maori fireside sing on a winter's night! I was struck, of course, how deeply New Zealand had become a part of us if even our children were delighting in using the language of the original inhabitants of this land that faces towards Antarctica.

More than that was my awareness as we tucked them into bed, that we were ending a year on the road. Almost to the day, one year ago we had picked up Caroline at the airport from visiting my mother in Florida, and, having sold our New Orleans home and moved all belongings to Oklahoma to be placed in storage, we had headed by car towards California. That led to our American journey, followed by five months in Europe, including the months on Kea.

We turned in that last night in Wellington surrounded by suitcases, a smoldering fire, happily sleeping children, and a wealth of memories of life on the road around the world. We wouldn't trade our mobile year for anything. Not every moment had been a pleasure, of course. In Maori terms, life is a necessary mixture of the "*tapu*"—the sacred—and the "*noa*"—ordinary or "every day." Travel had brought us doses of both, but the overall feeling as that last night suggests had been one of shared joy, and the pleasure of new friendships.

The floors of our house at 11 Moir Street were shining, the carpeting had been freshly cleaned, and the postcards from friends had been removed from the fridge door. In short, except for the mountain of suitcases in the front hall, the place looked like it did when we arrived in January exactly six months before.

Missions had been accomplished. I had even turned in *Make A Joyful Noise*, the jazz sheep farm comic script Russell Campbell and I had written. And I finished, early that last morning, reading the twenty-two feature screenplays my students turned in at the university during the last week. Hey, some were very good, and I helped point them towards film producers.

It was, however, time to move on.

Even Sam's skateboard had been carefully taken apart and packed.

That was serious. It was the mark of travelers about to head on out again.

As we closed the door to 11 Moir St and headed for the airport, I silently blew a kiss to both the TAPU and NOA in life and travels!

And yet before leaving there had been time for one last jog down to the harbor and around a pier where Maori and Samoan fishermen stood patiently morning after morning, with large fish being yanked out of the bay from time to time. The previous day I had done this loop and took a break from jogging when I saw too old Maoris seated on the pier with an ice bucket with a bottle of white wine sticking out of it. Instead of the usual beer bottle in a brown bag, they were sipping good Hawke's Bay white wine.

"How's it going?" I asked.

"The whole New Zealand economy is shit," said one sipping his early morning wine, well aware of my non-Kiwi accent, "But the fish are biting REAL GOOD!"

I smiled and kept on jogging.

CLOSING DOWN

The door to the Air New Zealand plane closed and a pang went through me. This was it. The very end of our year on the road as we headed back to New Orleans. I brushed away a few tears and thought about the lines from a story by Maori writer Patricia Grace:

> We gather. We sing and dance together for my going. We laugh and cry. We touch. We mingle tears as blood. I give you my farewell. ("And So I Go," p. 47)

For a brief moment we could see Wellington, its windy bay, and the rising hills around it as our plane climbed after lift off. But soon we had passed through the cloud level and Auckland, Los Angeles, and New Orleans lay ahead. And a new life awaited us all in Oklahoma.

ENDINGS AND NEW BEGINNINGS

Czech novelist Milan Kundera has a fitting final blessing for us all:

"I beg you, friend, be happy. I have the vague sense
That on your capacity to be happy hangs our only hope."

Slowness (p. 156)

For our year on the move, we had taken Kundera's command seriously. We had been happy, and, more times than we could imagine, very happy. No regrets and many fond memories. I write these words from our new life as residents of Norman, Oklahoma, from a two-story wooden home with a wide front porch in walking distance from the University of Oklahoma where both Odette and I work. And our home is walking distance to Sam and Caroline's schools and a corner deli that sells among everything else, the *New York Times*.

But an old Eskimo song comes to mind when thinking about our travelling year:

AN ESKIMO SONG
And I think over again
My small adventures
When with a shore wind I drifted out
In my kayak
And thought I was in danger.
My fears,
Those I thought so big,
For all the vital things
I had to get and to reach.

And yet, there is only
One great thing,
The only thing:
To live to see in huts and on journeys
The great day that dawns
And the light that fills the world.

Oklahoma is not an Eskimo territory. But it is very much the center of over thirty-five native American nations. And when soon after we had arrived in Norman, a native American colleague came to our home and performed a Cherokee "Smoking" ceremony to welcome us, we all realized that our travels had equipped us to enjoy and appreciate this new experience in the land (Okla) of red people (Homa).

Was it our journey that made settling into our new home so painless?

Perhaps.

On a balmy October evening three months after our arrival in Oklahoma, we were sitting around a campfire in a state park where we were camping. We had driven three hours north of Norman into Osage Indian territory, which we had visited before locating the park and our campsite. But we had now set up our tent on a huge hill overlooking forests and prairie grasslands beyond, full of bison. Before supper we had driven around the park seeing wild turkeys and deer jumping and waddling around, seemingly without fear of us. Then after a steak and couscous meal, Sam and Caroline were roasting marshmallows.

We thought back to a year before, which would have been on Kea, and our birthday weekend shared with friends as the weather began to turn chilly. A sigh and a question to Odette on that Oklahoma evening. A year on the road with the family: would you do it over again, given the chance?

"Absolutely!" was Odette's clear and joyful return.